L.I.F.E. Recovery Guide for Women

A Workbook for Living in Freedom Everyday in Sexual Wholeness and Integrity

Marnie C. Ferree

with core material by

Mark Laaser

Mark Laaser, Ph.D., Editor

*L.I.F.E. Recovery Guide*s for *L*iving *I*n *F*reedom *E*veryday

L.I.F.E. Recovery Guide for Women
by Marnie C. Ferree, M.A., LMFT

Printed in the United States of America

NOTE: This workbook is not intended to provide therapy, counseling, clinical advice or treatment, or to take the place of clinical advice and treatment from a professional mental health provider or personal physician. Readers are advised to consult qualified healthcare providers regarding mental, emotional and medical issues. Neither the publisher, the author, nor L.I.F.E. Recovery assumes any responsibility for any possible consequences from any reader's action or application of information in this workbook.

Color House Graphics
www.colorhousegraphics.com

L.I.F.E. Recovery Guide for Women
Table of Contents

L.I.F.E. Guide Principles (P) & Assignments (A)

First Assignments

Second Assignments

Foreword

from L.I.F.E. Recovery

Sexual dysfunction has become a common cancer within today's culture, and the church is certainly not exempt. The number of people struggling with sexual brokenness has sky-rocketed due to two main factors: the prevalence and availability of pornography, and a sexually saturated media. Mark Laaser has commented that our entire society is being sexually abused by this onslaught. Unhealthy and unscriptural sexual behaviors such as pornography, compulsive masturbation, and adultery are just as prevalent within the Christian community as they are in the society at large. Among believers, there are men and women - including key leaders - who, because of painful experiences and sinful choices, compulsively use sex and unholy relationships as an escape or medication to help them cope with life. Many of these same people desperately long to be free from their bondage and intensely desire to live in sexual integrity. They want to experience genuine L.I.F.E. - Living In Freedom Everyday.

This *L.I.F.E. Recovery Guide for Women* is the second in a series of workbooks dedicated to helping God's people be free from the bondage of sexual addiction and equipping them to walk in His unconditional love. L.I.F.E. Recovery is proud to have Dr. Mark Laaser, an internationally known author and leader in the area of sexual addiction recovery, overseeing the creation of these workbooks. **Dr. Laaser conceptualized the Seven Principles of being Faithful and True and wrote the core teaching material found in each workbook. A respected expert in a specific area of ministry, such as women, spouses, etc., adapted the material for that target population. This design provides consistency of information and terminology throughout the *L.I.F.E. Recovery Guide* series.**

The L.I.F.E. Recovery support group program offers Christ-centered and relationally oriented groups that incorporate spiritual discipline, small group accountability, and ongoing prayer and support for those struggling with sexual brokenness. L.I.F.E. Recovery Groups are support groups, not therapy groups. While there is much within each of the *L.I.F.E. Recovery Guide*s and the recommended recovery materials to help the struggler identify and deal with the wounds from the past, we also encourage individual therapy to address root issues that often lead to sexual addiction. Healing this core woundedness is vital to living in freedom everyday, and most people need the help of a trained counselor.

The ongoing support so critical to the process of transformation comes from the networking of lives through L.I.F.E. Recovery Groups. These groups involve real relationships - open, transparent, and accountable connections with fellow strugglers. L.I.F.E. Recovery Groups value confidentiality and maintain an absolute commitment to provide a safe atmosphere for complete honesty and complete acceptance, where members are embraced in an attitude of love and forgiveness from others sharing common struggles. All of these components "guide" the group members toward Christ-centered sexuality, according to the conviction that our true sexual identity is found in the freedom and grace that only Jesus can offer.

Foreword

by Mark Laaser, Ph.D.

Welcome to the journey toward *Living In Freedom Everyday*. I pray that this workbook will richly bless your life. Producing it has been a labor of love and is the result of the wisdom and generosity of many people, including the hundreds of addicts and spouses I've had the honor of working with over the years. But, mostly, this *L.I.F.E. Recovery Guide* is the product of God's love and grace in many lives, including my own.

The foundation of this workbook and the others in this L.I.F.E. series rests on my "Seven Principles of Being Faithful and True." These were originally conceived when I worked with the American Family Association in 1997. The title, "Faithful and True," was taken from my first book and companion workbook.[i] It resulted from a conversation I had with Gary Smalley about conceptualizing a more positive way of looking at the struggle involved in achieving or maintaining sexual fidelity. The name "Faithful and True" recognizes that all Christian women and men seek to be sexually whole or pure.

Those familiar with the Twelve Steps of Alcoholics Anonymous will recognize that the Principles follow the outline of those steps. I have always believed that the Twelve Steps contain much wisdom, but many Christians have been reluctant to use them because they aren't specific enough about our need to be in a totally dependent relationship with Christ. To meet this goal, I elaborated on the language of the Twelve Steps in a way that is consistent with our faith. I also made some logical pairings that condensed the Steps into Seven Principles.

The Journey of Transformation

This workbook also introduces a new way of looking at what has for years been called "**recovery**." This term describes the journey of freedom from old behaviors. It is somewhat a misnomer, though, because we don't seek to recover old ways. Who wants to go back to the way things were? But, we *do* seek to "recover" in that we *want to get well*. This "wellness" or freedom that we seek, however, is more accurately a matter of "**transformation**." It is a journey that involves changing our lives – an accomplishment that is achieved through God's transforming power and love. Many of you familiar with the language of the recovery movement will notice some ways that words change when we think of the healing journey as "transforming." This terminology is rich with meaning and theology that the language of "recovery" lacks. It best conveys both the nature of the journey itself and the power of the Transformer, who makes us into "new creatures" alive in Him.

Registration with L.I.F.E. Recovery

We encourage all groups using this L.I.F.E. Recovery Guide to ***Register your L.I.F.E. Recovery Group***. Registering your L.I.F.E. Recovery Group with L.I.F.E. Recovery International ensures effective recovery literacy through the time tested best practices shown in the LRM, the L.I.F.E. Recovery Model (http://www.freedomeveryday.org/lrm/index.php). Registration also entitles your group facilitator to access discounts on workbooks and opens communication links for information about conferences, workshops, and leadership and ministry training. Through newsletters and the L.I.F.E. Recovery website, your group facilitators will have access to materials and information to help your L.I.F.E. Recovery Group grow and to expand your recovery ministry within your church and your community. Registered L.I.F.E. Recovery Groups will also be listed in our network of L.I.F.E. Recovery Groups, so those looking for help in your community can find it, and your group members will never be without needed support when away from home. Finally, by registering, one by one, groups will be furthering the work of L.I.F.E. Recovery International helping to make this support group ministry available in additional churches and communities across the country and around the world.

To find out more information, to start a L.I.F.E. Recovery Group, or to become a Registered L.I.F.E. Recovery Group, checkout the ministry's website, call toll-free, or write for more information. We would love to welcome you and start you on the journey toward *Living In Freedom Everyday* in God's unconditional love.

L.I.F.E. Recovery International   **866-408-LIFE (866-408-5433)**
P.O. Box 952317
Lake Mary, FL 32795

www.freedomeveryday.org

---

[i] Mark R. Laaser, *Faithful and True* (Zondervan, Grand Rapids, MI) 1996; *Faithful and True Workbook* (Lifeway Press, Nashville, TN) 1996.

Healthy Intimacy, Recovery and Grieving

Patrick Carnes PhD, a pioneer in addiction recovery, states "more than 87 percent of addicts come from disengaged families — a family environment in which family members are detached, uninvolved, or emotionally absent. *All compulsive and addictive behaviors are signs of significant intimacy disorder and the inability to get needs met in healthy ways.*" Carnes' statement suggests the importance of being connected, involved and emotionally present in order to get our needs met in healthy ways and since this hasn't been modeled we have to learn how this is done. There are three critical elements that promote this growth: managing distressing emotions, support and disclosure and cognitive processing. Each are satisfied in a L.I.F.E. Recovery Group setting where a person learns to express feelings relating to an injury including anger, anxiety, and sadness and processing that pain. In reality, this is grief work. A fundamental part of your recovery journey is learning to cooperate with the grieving process, i.e. expressing your feelings and processing pain. This central idea is why the L.I.F.E. Grieving Guide has been created for anyone struggling with any compulsive and addictive behavior so everyone can *Live In Freedom Everyday.*

Statement of Faith

L.I.F.E. Recovery International believes that the Scriptures of the Old and New Testaments are completely inspired by God and should be the single authority for instructions in healthy and godly living. We believe in one God who exists in three persons - the Father, the Son, and the Holy Spirit. We believe that Jesus Christ is the only begotten Son of the Father, and that He was conceived by the Holy Spirit, born of the Virgin Mary, and lived a sinless life. He was crucified and buried and rose from the dead to sit at the right hand of the Father. He will come again to the earth in power and glory. We believe that only through true faith in Jesus Christ as Savior and Lord can a person enter the Kingdom of Heaven. We believe that God's Holy Spirit empowers us to grow closer to our Heavenly Father and to obediently walk in His will.

We further believe that a successful recovery journey requires transformation based on the principles in this L.I.F.E. Recovery Guide and the surrender of your life to Jesus Christ.

The *L.I.F.E. Recovery Guide for Women*

Women who struggle with sexual addiction have historically been overlooked by those who provide recovery material or offer support groups. Stereotypically, sex addicts are presumed to be male. This gender "discrimination" surrounding sexual addiction recovery prompts a great need for new material and groups designed specifically for women. To my knowledge, this *L.I.F.E. Recovery Guide* is the first workbook written specifically for female sex addicts. Only *one* book, in fact, directs information and healing toward the female sex addict, at least from a sound clinical base coupled with a Christian perspective. The material offered here is explored in depth in Marnie Ferree's book *No Stones: Women Redeemed From Sexual Shame*,[ii] which would be a helpful companion to this *L.I.F.E. Recovery Guide*. (Ordering information for *No Stones: Women Redeemed from Sexual Shame* is detailed in the back of this workbook).

Likewise, female sex addicts experience great difficulty in finding a support group. While the major secular Twelve Step fellowships include women, I am not aware of any "Faithful and True" or Christian support groups for women only. In fact, most Christian recovery groups for sexual addiction *exclude* women. Female Christian addicts are simply not allowed to attend. Whether from ignorance, fear, or discomfort, Christian-based support groups for sex addiction are usually solely for males.

I am grateful that God called Marnie Ferree to minister to these women who had no voice or leader. I met Marnie over a decade ago, and as she progressed in her own journey of transformation, I watched her embark on a career focused on helping other women who struggle with sexual sin and addiction. Today Marnie is the undisputed leader in the field of women's sexual addiction recovery, and she is highly respected in both the secular and Christian communities. Her heart is tender toward women who long for grace and guidance as they seek to live in sexual wholeness and purity. Her authorship of this *L.I.F.E. Recovery Guide for Women* is further evidence of how Marnie allows God to "redeem" her pain, which is the way she describes her work. Deb and I are grateful to know Marnie and David and to share in joint ministry efforts and meaningful friendship.

As editor of these *L.I.F.E. Recovery Guides*, my prayer is that this *L.I.F.E. Recovery Guide for Women,* as well as all the other workbooks in the series, will richly benefit and empower your life as you seek to *L*ive *I*n *F*reedom *E*veryday through the grace of Jesus Christ.

[ii] Marnie C. Ferree, *No Stones: Women Redeemed From Sexual Shame* (Xulon Press, Fairfax, VA) 2002.

Author's Acknowledgements

Though most creative efforts involve a number of people, this *L.I.F.E. Recovery Guide for Women* is an unusually cooperative venture. The most credit belongs to Dr. Mark Laaser, a long-time colleague and leader in this field. In fact, complete accuracy would list his name along with mine as the author, because Mark wrote much of the core material contained in this *Guide*. In effect, I simply adapted his writing to suit a feminine audience. In many places the manuscripts are identical, and this final product is largely a duplication-with-a few-adaptations of the *L.I.F.E. Recovery Guide for Men*. Mark conceived this design for the workbook series and this *Guide* is produced with his blessing as editor, but I want to give credit where credit is due. (One of the principles of my program is to practice rigorous honesty.) It's my privilege to collaborate with Mark in this workbook series.

It is also my joy to pool resources with Johna and Bob Hale and L.I.F.E. Recovery International. This workbook series has been their vision for a long time, and they've steadily kept on the path until its completion. Their big hearts and many gifts are poured freely into hurting lives with unusual tenderness and tenacity. They have encouraged me in this project and patiently waited while it took much longer to complete than I intended.

L.I.F.E. Recovery Guide
The energy for this work comes from the hundreds of female sex addicts who have been a part of my journey, both as clients and as sisters on the same path to wholeness. I thank you for your courage and for all you've taught me about honesty, perseverance, and humility.

Most of all, the grace (in human terms) to complete this work has come from my husband David. No one could ask for a more supportive spouse. On a daily basis David practices the grace and transformation that I preach. His forgiveness and love allow us to walk in freedom everyday from the bondage of our past. David's gentle spirit and generous heart are amazing gifts I could never deserve.

At the risk of appearing trite, I must give the ultimate acknowledgement to my holy father God. Only a loving God could coax me into this journey of transformation, and only God could empower me to *Live In Freedom Everyday*. To Him be all the glory!

Introduction
by Marnie C. Ferree, M.A.

For years women battling sexual sin have desperately needed a safe place to connect with each other, to learn from and encourage each other, and to support each other in the journey of transformation. *Praise God that now group material is available specifically for women*! I'm honored and humbled to have a part in the creation of this *L.I.F.E. Recovery Guide*. I pray Christian women who struggle with sexual addiction will soon be meeting in groups all across the country to share their experience, strength, and hope.

My Story: A Woman Redeemed

This workbook really begins with my own story of sexual sin and addiction. It starts when I was three years old and my mother died from cancer. The story continues through the powerful impact my father had on my life, in both positive and negative ways. A critical piece is the sexual abuse I experienced by a dear family friend (a father figure), which significantly shaped my thoughts and behavior. Beginning at age five and continuing until my late teens, this man taught me that sex equals love, that significant relationships are supposed to be sexual, that I could use my sexuality to control and manipulate, and that no one would protect or nurture me but myself. It was decades later, at the age of 35, before I understood that most of his instruction was full of lies.

By that time my first marriage had ended in divorce because of my infidelities, and my second marriage was fast heading in that direction. My young children were affected in ways I didn't imagine. My sexual addiction, which began in my teens, was totally out of control. It had ruined my relationships with my family, my self-esteem, and my health. Eventually, I was diagnosed with cervical cancer caused by a sexually transmitted disease, and I nearly died from complications of surgery.

Most importantly, my addiction had broken my connection with God. Though my body finally healed from my physical disease, I knew I remained horribly sick spiritually. But my spiritual illness, not surprisingly, was secret. In my double life, I was very active in church. I taught Sunday School, sang in the choir, and published inspirational Christian essays. I spoke frequently at local women's groups and hosted a women's Bible study. On the outside, I looked like I had it all together. On the inside, I was a total wreck.

By God's grace, I ultimately reached a point where I could no longer live with the extreme duality of my life. I often say that I was in too much pain to go on living, but I was too afraid to die. In my suicidal despair, I finally dared to ask for help. That desperate plea set me on a journey I could not have imagined. A wise Christian counselor and a handful of recovering friends took my hands and led me through the early years of transformation. My husband stuck with me, forgave me, and embarked on his own journey of recovery. In God's transforming power and grace, I've received a new life and a new focus, including professionally as well as personally.

Today I am humbled and blessed by twenty years of healing and transformation from sexual behaviors outside of my marriage. David and I have been married since 1981, and our now-grown children and grandchildren enjoy a much healthier family. I work professionally in the field of sexual addiction recovery, which for me is a way to redeem the pain. I'm privileged to write and speak about God's grace, healing, and transforming power. When I share, I often use elements of my own story to illustrate various points. I don't disclose about my experiences to show you how wonderful I am to have stopped my sexually sinful behaviors. It's only through the transforming power and love of God that I am even alive. I use my own story in the hope that you'll be encouraged in knowing that *I am one of you*. A loving, holy Father refused to stone me in my sin, and instead, brought me out of the pit into a new way of life. As Mark Laaser explains, I don't write from some distant academic place, but from the depth of gratitude in my soul. Like you, I'm also deeply longing for a more dependent relationship with Jesus Christ as I continue to seek Him and know Him more fully.

Most of all, I share because I want you to know that healing *is* possible. When I began my own journey, I thought God was finished with me. I truly believed God would reject me because of my sexual sins. Likewise, I fully expected rejection from my family and friends. I had hurt too many people; including those I loved the most. My marriage was dissolving; my children were wounded and angry. It was only then, in that total brokenness, that I truly began to find the reality and healing presence of a loving, forgiving, restoring God. In my total weakness, God continued to pursue me. Eventually, I came to understand a key promise of Alcoholics Anonymous: *God will do for me what I cannot do for myself.* During those early challenging years of my journey, I clung to a promise recorded in Philippians 1:6: *"He who began a good work in you will be faithful to complete it."* And God has been faithful, indeed, beyond my wildest dreams, which answers a prayer recorded in Ephesians 3: 17b-21, another Scripture I read countless times. David and I eventually embarked together on a journey to transform our hearts and our relationship, and today we're blessed beyond measure.

In the middle of my sickness and brokenness, I never thought I'd be writing a book like this one. (I'd written plenty of Christian material that wasn't backed up with integrity in my life. I didn't think I could ever have credibility.) But God has done many unexpected things in these ensuing years, including the chance to prepare this workbook for hurting women who fear they'll be stoned, rather than helped, by their Christian community.

I hope, dear one, that you find this *L.I.F.E. Recovery Guide* a significant help in your journey of healing and transformation. It's another way God is allowing me to "comfort others as I have been comforted" (2 Corinthians 1:3). Please know that even as I write, I'm praying for you, and for you to know God in a more personal and powerful way as Christ completes the good work He has begun in your life.

Marnie

An Introduction
To the Addictive Condition

SPIRITUAL DOCTRINE: If God can heal disease then He can heal me!

As a Christian, you may be wondering why you should submit yourself to a "man-made" recovery program.   Why not, instead, spend your time praying for an instantaneous deliverance brought about by an outpouring of Gods power? After all, the Bible speaks of the POWER of the Holy Spirit that works within you, the Bible says that God did not give you a spirit of fear but of POWER, the Bible says that the same POWER that raised Jesus from the dead resides inside you...so why the need for a PROCESS?

Well, this is a very fair question with a very simple answer. The truth is, nearly every addict that comes to our ministry has been praying intensely and often for God to deliver them from their addiction. This is a good thing to do and therefore it is something we encourage. God DOES pour out His power to bring healing to addicts.   His power to heal addictions, however, does not strike once like a lightning bolt; it flows continually like a river. It is a power that can only be experienced through simple, authentic Christian fellowship.   It requires the conduits of transparency, confession, debriefing, and relearning - all of which can only be experienced through community. So it's not a question of power vs. process; it's an embracing of God's power *through* process.

God often heals cancer and other physical ailments instantaneously because doing so does not compromise the overall health of our physical body. In the case of addiction, however, an instantaneous healing *would* compromise our overall emotional and mental health. Such an experience would teach us that our deepest emotional conflicts (which are at the core of our addictive condition) can be healed in isolation and this is not possible. This would be a lesson that is counter-productive to God's design for us, as He has created us for intimacy – with Himself, with His Son Jesus and with each other. We were wounded in relationship; therefore God has chosen to bring healing through relationship. Of course He could bring instant relief of the craving, but years of experience and biblical evidence indicates that He has chosen to bring wholeness through our active participation in a transparent Christian community. If in this transparent environment we address core wounds that have hindered our spiritual maturity we will remove the tendency to switch addictions altogether. We will talk more about this later. Meanwhile, welcome to a L.I.F.E. Time of recovery!

FAMILY SYSTEMS: This looks familiar...

If there is one thing you need to understand about addiction it's this: Coping or self-medicating doesn't need an invitation...it only needs an opportunity.

At one time, you were an innocent, unsuspecting child. You, most likely, weren't guided through the experiences in your life that opened the door for a need to escape. Your family, much like any other, may have been unreliable and unskilled themselves to bear the challenge of making it through the day's circumstances. Maybe the best model you saw was how to simply survive. Perhaps you learned at an early age that life cannot be trusted to turn out well so you made your way through the turmoil by using any opportunity to cope and escape the reality. Yet this was your home, your family, your relationships and extended family. In fact, there is an entire psychological discipline about this. It was originally formulated by Dr. Murray Bowen and is called **family systems theory**. As Dr. Bowen explains,

> *A family is a system in which each member has a role to play and rules to respect. Members of the system are expected to respond to each other in a certain way according to their role, which is determined by relationship agreements. Within the boundaries of the system, patterns develop as certain family member's behavior is caused by and causes other family member's behaviors in predictable ways.*

In short, Dr. Bowen believed that you, as a person, cannot be understood (or understand yourself) apart from your family system. This is true because of the following widely recognized principle: early influences operate to shape future behavior. And the majority of your early influences came to you through your family system. Unfortunately, the chaos and injury some of us experienced within our family systems set us up to be vulnerable to compulsive and addictive behavior as adults. Some family systems can even go so far as *modeling* this type of behavior for us! You can see scriptural reference in Exodus 20 for this type of generational curse. Is it any wonder that our addictive condition looks familiar?

FRAGMENTATION: I think I'm going mad…

Your dependency can certainly be driving you to **fragmentation.** According to Christopher J. Charleton, M.A., LCSW, a licensed clinical therapist and president of InterAct Counseling PLLC, a state-of-the-art Christian treatment facility in Rochester, NY, fragmentation is a result of disintegration, which is in direct contrast to God's design of integration. That sounds a bit confusing to me, so think of it this way: you were created in the image of the Triune God; God the Father, God the Son and God the Holy Spirit. The Trinity is a perfect example of integration; each aspect of the trinity is in union with the others, glorifying and reflecting each other's true value in relationship. Similarly, as someone created in God's image you were also designed to be integrated in relationships, thereby illuminating the true value of yourself and others.

The problem is your family of origin experiences challenged your belief in God's design and skewed your perception of the value of being integrated in community. When your relationships were subsequently compromised (or even avoided altogether), disintegration occurred. Now, here's the main point: **fragmentation perceives both integration and disintegration to be true**…and an internal war between intimacy and isolation ensues. The apostle Paul said it this way, "I don't understand what I do. For what I want to do (intimacy) I don't do, and the very thing I hate (isolation) I do. Now if I do what I do not want to do it is no longer I who does it, but it is sin (dependency) living in me" (additions mine). So then, this L.I.F.E. Guide you're holding, its Principles and Journal Assignments will prove to be a huge benefit by giving you the tools to examine yourself and your experiences. After all, don't we want to live in freedom? It's our skewed perception that fuels the war between intimacy and isolation in the first place.

ADDICTIVE CONDITION: So one more time… What's my problem?

It's not alcohol. Alcohol does not create alcoholics. It's not pornography. Pornography doesn't create sex addicts. Neither is your addictive condition a box of Twinkies or a deck of cards or a freshly rolled joint or an eighty hour a week job.

The problem is your underlying addictive *condition* and it consists of a whole host of issues; neurochemical imbalances, arrested development, unresolved emotional wounds, fragmentation, and an incapacity for emotional wholeness and intimacy. These are the things that create addicts. The problem does not resemble a pair of dice, a sexual encounter, or a box of chocolates, although it likes to play with things like these - especially when you are in pain. Given enough pain and enough opportunity, these things then become the focus of your addictive *behavior.*

In recovery terms, your addictive behavior is simply your attempt to medicate the pain of some past trauma or relational wounding that has not been resolved, and the fact that it remains unresolved becomes the (often subconscious) excuse for continuing in your addictive behavior. It is a self-perpetuating cycle of destruction. And on top of that, Satan is always there to cooperate, using and intensifying your addictive behavior and further disabling your ability to have relationships with those you care about (or even with God Himself). Your problem, your addictive condition, is your enemy and is used by the enemy to bring devastation to your life. Nevertheless, your addictive condition, your coping method or self-medicating always masquerades as your friend.

You very likely found your method(s) of coping amidst the turmoil of your family system. Acting out was fun and even helpful at first, but as you continually fed your addictive condition through years the behavior became pretty burdensome. And so you're here, in need of a community of people who can help you to more clearly identify what's driving your addictive condition and help you through God's healing power to uncover and heal those wounds, for good!

Oh…so what you are really saying is I just need to get sober.

Nope.

Huh?

Sobriety is measured in time. You will be deemed "sober" when you have not engaged in addictive behaviors for twenty-four hours, or a week, a month, etc. That's a great start, but it is not enough.

Your addictive condition is clever, resourceful and sinister, and it will let you be sober for a while if it means it can hang around for the long haul. Even Satan, after unsuccessfully tempting Jesus in the desert, simply waited for a more opportune time. Your addictive condition will do the same.

What you need is wholeness. Sobriety is a part of the equation but by itself sobriety does not equal wholeness. Being whole means you are practicing real intimacy. It means you are self-aware and capable of modulating negative emotions through healthy means. It means you are present in the moment instead of being lost inside your head. It means you no longer hide behind "fine." Being whole means God is having His way with you, and as a result you are being transformed inside and out. The point is, you can be sober and still be acting out of your addictive condition. But when you are whole your addictive condition is not only *not* driving - but has no opportunity to re-establish itself and get a seat within you.

By joining a local L.I.F.E. Recovery Group and completing the work that is found in the L.I.F.E. Recovery Guide you are holding, we believe you can achieve wholeness. Accomplishing this will require a lot of consistent effort on your part, but know this; there are thousands of men and women throughout the world who can give testimony to the fact that it was the community and self-discovery they found through L.I.F.E. Recovery that God used to set them free. You **can** live in freedom everyday! Welcome to L.I.F.E.!

How to Use This *L.I.F.E. Recovery Guide*

Hopefully, you'll use this workbook because someone at a L.I.F.E. Recovery Group recommended it. You've made a decision to do something about your sexual addiction and have found a L.I.F.E. Group, which means you'll have the strength of the fellowship of other women to help you get started. Lean on them and learn how to listen. (Realize that your own best thinking got you here. Open yourself to learning a different way.) Quiet your mind. Remind Satan that he's lost the battle with you and should just shut up and leave you alone. You don't want to listen to him, because you're recognizing he's the father of lies. Make a firm commitment *not* to listen to him again.

Your Private Journal

The first thing you'll need to do is get a journal of some sort. It could be as simple as a spiral bound notebook, or it could be a fancy journal you can find at bookstores and office supply stores. It may even be a three-ring binder so that you can add as many pages as you need. Whatever its form, your personal journal should be something you feel completely comfortable writing in. The leaders of L.I.F.E. Recovery made a decision not to put a great deal of space in this workbook for you to write in so that you can refer back to this material over and over again. You may copy some of the pages and give them to others. The plan is for you to do most of the writing assignments in your journal instead of in this workbook, but sometimes you'll notice short-answer space is provided for convenience. Each assignment contains some discussion about the Principle being presented and the thought processes necessary to complete the particular writing assignment(s) within that Principle. The actual assignment instructions are clearly marked within the discussion content to be sure it's evident what you should record in your journal.

Be certain to put your name on your journal. It will become *your* **sacred** document, and no one else should see it unless *you* decide to share it. Do you remember how some old diaries had locks on them to protect the contents? Get that idea in your mind. This is your journal for you to record your answers and thoughts with complete honesty. We don't want anyone else reading it uninvited.

I've observed over the years that others may want to look at your journal. Your husband will probably be one of them. Don't be hard on him for wanting to see what you've written. He's petrified and hurt. He wants to know the truth. He's angry with you and feels he has the right to read your journal.

But believe me: **It's a healthy boundary to keep private the contents of this diary about your life**. Don't be afraid to set this boundary. (Another important suggestion is to keep your journal out of plain sight, so that others aren't unnecessarily tempted to invade your privacy.) *The writing that you do in your journal is between you and God.* Pray for the power of the Holy Spirit to help you be honest and thorough and to guard your writings from unauthorized eyes.

You may at times want to show what you've written to your husband, to others, to your sponsor, group members, pastor, or therapist. That choice is acceptable if you decide it's for *your* benefit. But please know that's *your* decision, OK? Refuse to be pressured into sharing your journal, especially by your spouse

Organization of L.I.F.E. Recovery Guide Material

Each of the Seven Principles is divided into three assignments. Every time a L.I.F.E. Recovery Group meets it will focus on one of the seven Principles as the theme for that meeting. Each L.I.F.E. Recovery Group, though, will be attended by members who are at different stages in their healing journey. Some may have years of sobriety, while others may be coming to their first meeting. **L.I.F.E. Recovery Groups should always be open to new members who are coming for the first time**. No one can predict God's timing about when a person may finally decide to seek help. Therefore, every time a L.I.F.E. Recovery Group focuses on a Principle, each person in the group should be working one of the three assignments within that Principle.

Each assignment is designed to take you deeper in the work of a Principle. Assignment One consistently is somewhat basic — it's the core and the foundation of that Principle. Each Assignment Two asks you to work on the next core elements. Finally, Assignment Three takes you into deeper understandings of a Principle.

L.I.F.E. Recovery Guide Assignment Flow

The flow of the L.I.F.E. Recovery Guide assignments is such that you'll work on the assignments in succession as formatted in this L.I.F.E. Recovery Guide. The plan is that you'll work on all <u>seven of the first assignments first</u>, then all seven of the <u>second</u> assignments, and finally all seven of the <u>third</u> assignments. This schedule means that after completing Principle One, Assignment One, you'll move on to Principle <u>Two</u>, Assignment One. When you've completed Principle Seven, Assignment One, you'll begin Principle One, Assignment <u>Two</u>, as arranged in this workbook.

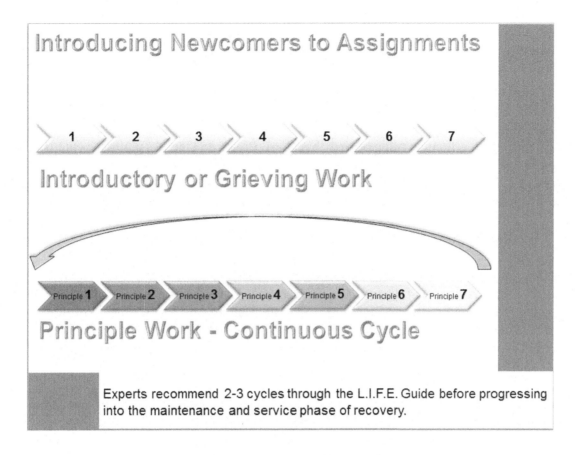

For the purpose of clarifying the introduction of newcomers to L.I.F.E. Recovery Guide assignments, Dr. Laaser writes the following statement.

> *"We've always suggested that all participants be on the same principle*
> *yet they can be on different assignments."*

As suggested by Dr. Laaser, the main group continually cycles through Principles 1-7 emphasizing all levels of assignments relevant to the participants that are present. Because newcomers are asked to complete introductory work before beginning the L.I.F.E. Guide assignments, the following approach illustrates our recommendation to introduce participants to the workbook assignments, please read the following.

Orientation or Grieving Guide - Introductory Work:
Unless there are other attendees in the Introductory Group, the newcomer works independently on those assignments while attending the main Principle group, which then allows for the discussion of their homework in small group. After completion of Introductory work, the newcomer then begins the Principle work in the main group.

Principle Work (Main Group):
Although the newcomer attends the main Principle group without interruption, due to the foundation building aspect of the L.I.F.E. Recovery Guide assignments and the continuous cycle of the Principles in the main group, the newcomer should take this opportunity to

journal and observe the group and wait to begin the material when the group cycles back to Principle 1.

Working through the Principles

Remember that you'll be working **across** this chart. Principle One, Assignment One is where you begin. Principle Seven, Assignment One is the seventh work you do. Principle One, Assignment Two is the eighth work. Principle One, Assignment Three is the fifteenth. Finally, Principle Seven, Assignment Three is the twenty-first work you complete.

There are a total, then, of twenty-one assignments. This outline doesn't necessarily mean you'll only need 21 weeks to go through the *L.I.F.E. Recovery Guide*. It may take you several weeks to do just one of the assignments. Work at a pace that's comfortable for you. *Being thorough is more important than being quick.* Your sponsor or your group can help you know how you're doing. Remember that at each meeting you'll be working on an assignment related to the Principle being discussed that night. This format technically means you could work several different times on the same assignment in a Principle, but that those times could be seven weeks apart.

Let's assume, for example, that you're working on Principle One, Assignment One. You start on this lesson the first time your L.I.F.E. Recovery Group is addressing that Principle. The next week you move to Principle Two, Assignment One. You may not be completely finished with Principle One, Assignment One, and that's fine. You can come back to it later. At this point, you just keep going through the *L.I.F.E. Recovery Guide* and move on to Principle Two so that you'll be on task with the others. When the group cycles back to Principle One after seven weeks, you take up where you left off in Assignment One. Following this slower format might take you a year to work through the entire workbook for the first time. That's fine. Others of you may want to march right through and get all the work of an assignment done in one week, which means you'll go through the entire workbook during the first 21 weeks. Everyone is different. Recovery isn't a race or a competition; it's a transforming way of life.

This *L.I.F.E. Recovery Guide* is a living, breathing document. You may work through it a number of times in the course of your healing journey. In fact, I hope you will. The inventory you complete in Principle Four, for example, will expand as you grow in your journey of self-awareness and honesty. It will be more complete when you have several years of sobriety as compared to when you're just starting out in recovery.

Your L.I.F.E. Recovery Group will concentrate on the Seven Principles of transformation. My hope is that all the exercises in this Guide will challenge you. Some of them may overwhelm you. There's a tremendous amount of work outlined in these pages. At times you may be tempted to skip some exercises or skimp on writing your answers. I pray you'll persevere and complete each assignment. **A key point to remember is that rigorous and thorough work is the best way to start healing.**

You may discover you fill more than one journal as you go through this material. Good for you! Journaling is one of the best emotional and spiritual tools available, and working in this *L.I.F.E. Recovery Guide* may be your start of this wonderful spiritual discipline. (Many great writers journal regularly.) As you read and study Scripture for the rest of your life, writing your thoughts and feelings may become like a friend that helps you grow continually.

As you'll notice, there are other suggested readings along the way, which are intended to be helpful in your work here. I certainly don't claim that this effort is "exhaustive." It's the most complete workbook I'm aware of, but it's only one book. More and more, various ministries are publishing similar materials. Don't think you have to be "loyal" only to this *L.I.F.E. Recovery Guide.* A workbook is a tool which is designed for your benefit. If there are other materials that help with your transformation process, that's great. Use them to support your journey to freedom and healing.

Please don't hesitate to call someone at L.I.F.E. Recovery International if you find you don't understand an assignment. You can also ask another "sister" who has been working a recovery program for some time to help you. Your local group should give you a list of phone numbers for group members. As you progress, you'll become more comfortable with the practice of asking for help.

Most of all, I pray that the God of all peace and understanding will keep your heart and mind focused on Christ Jesus throughout this journey.

L.I.F.E. Recovery Group Meeting Guide

Identity of Groups

Because this series of workbooks is sponsored by L.I.F.E. Recovery, most of the support groups which use this material will call their groups "L.I.F.E. Recovery Groups." There may be other groups that use this material, such as the network of "Faithful and True" groups which have developed across the country. Some of those groups may choose to identify themselves by that or another name, but I encourage groups to become a L.I.F.E. Recovery Group in order to help support this work across the country and around the world. What your group calls itself isn't as important as *how* you conduct your meeting. All groups calling themselves "L.I.F.E." or "Faithful and True," and certainly all groups using this material, should follow these meeting guidelines and leadership principles. For the remainder of this chapter, I'll refer to groups as "L.I.F.E. Recovery Groups."

Christian therapists could use the material in these *L.I.F.E. Recovery Guides* to conduct a therapy group. In such cases, the meeting guide may not be necessary, as therapists will know how to competently conduct a group. **An important principle, however, is that L.I.F.E. Recovery doesn't encourage individuals to use this material alone, without being part of a group.** As you'll see, this work is intended to be done in fellowship, not in isolation. That intention doesn't mean, of course, that you won't do the specific exercises in most of the assignments alone. They're meant, though, to be processed with others in some form of accountability.

Group Format

Every L.I.F.E. Recovery Group should follow a standard format. Experience indicates that meetings that don't use a standard format can easily become free-for-alls. They're vulnerable to the moods and distractions of the moment. They're also vulnerable to the more dominant personalities in the group. (Many times those who seek to dominate are the least healthy ones in the group.) All groups need strong leadership, and a few individuals in every group will provide that. It's not fair to them, though, if only one or two always have to lead the group. **If the safety guidelines and meeting format listed below are followed, most of the issues about leadership and dominating individuals are eliminated.**

L.I.F.E. Recovery recommends the following outline. Each group or leader may modify the outline to best suit the group's unique needs, but *groups should modify with care*, because once the format is established, a group should stick to it consistently.

Consider duplicating the Meeting Format and the various Readings and laminating them or placing them in sheet protectors for ease of use during meetings.

L.I.F.E. Recovery Group Meeting Format
(Note: Italics provide instructions or information not intended to be read aloud.)

1. Opening Introduction and Prayer

Opening statement by the group leader:
    "My name is _____, and I am healing from sexual addiction. This is the *(state the time of the meeting, e.g. the Monday night)* **L.I.F.E. Recovery Group and I welcome each woman here. I commend you on your commitment to be sexually and relationally pure before God. This is a closed meeting, which means that only those seeking their own personal recovery may attend."**

Opening prayer: *The leader prays or the group joins in saying a prayer of their choosing, such as the Serenity Prayer or the Lord's Prayer.*

2. Group Introductions

Leader says:
    "I invite everyone to introduce herself as we go around the room."
Each woman introduces herself as the leader did:
    "My name is _____, and I am healing from sexual addiction."
A newcomer may choose to say:
    "My name is _____, and I'm a newcomer."

3. Welcome New Members

L.I.F.E. Recovery Groups are always open to new members or attendees who are seeking help. The leader says:
    "Is anyone attending a meeting for your first time? *(Pause for show of hands.)* **We welcome newcomers and we're glad you've come. At your first meeting you aren't expected to talk, but we'll be honored if you do. There may be opportunities for you to share either in this larger group session or after we break up into smaller groups. But most importantly, this is a time for you as a newcomer to listen and start feeling safe.**
    "We believe an important practice for everyone on the journey of transformation is to use a sponsor to help work this program. If you'd like a temporary sponsor for the next week(s), see me after the meeting. Also, if you have any questions about our L.I.F.E. Recovery Group and how it functions, please see me after the meeting."

4. Readings

Standard readings, which are printed in the L.I.F.E. Recovery Guide after this "Meeting Format" section, are shared at every meeting. The leader selects readers and distributes the readings before the meeting starts, if possible.
The leader says, **"I've asked** *(name)* **_____ to read the** *(name of reading)* **_____."**

Those who have agreed to read share the material below:

> **Mission Statement** *(or a part of the Mission Statement) - and/or -*
> **The Seven Principles**   *- and/or -*
> **The Seven "Cs"**   *- and/or -*
> **Safety Guidelines** *(always read if newcomers are present)*

5. Offering

An offering container is passed around the group as the leader says:
"There are no dues or fees for membership, and all are welcome regardless of their ability to make a contribution, but we do suggest that you make a meaningful weekly contribution as an investment in your own healing.   L.I.F.E. Recovery Groups are self-supporting; we pay for our own materials, rent *(if applicable)* **and other expenses, plus we send half of your contributions on to L.I.F.E. Recovery to ensure that others will have access to the kind of help you've found.   Alcoholics Anonymous would not have grown into the source of help to alcoholics worldwide without such regular contributions from its members."**

6. Business

The leader leads the group in any discussion of old and new business. Old business includes matters such as meeting times and places, and ordering of materials. New business includes matters such as special but related events outside of the group, or any announcement of matters pertaining to the group's well-being.

Note that all decisions are made through the consensus of group members and must be consistent with the policies of L.I.F.E. Recovery. When in doubt, check with the national office.

The leader says:
"Is there any old business we need to discuss?   (*pause***)
"Is there any new business or announcements that affect the group as a whole?"**

7. Discussion of Principle

By prior arrangement, someone will have been asked to either make a presentation or lead a discussion on the Principle being considered that night. This presentation should be limited to no more than 20 minutes.

The leader says:
"*(Name of member)* _____ **will now lead us in discussing Principle** *(number)* _____, **which is** _____ *(read text of Principle)* _____**."**

8. Small Group Discussion

Dividing into Groups:
This is a time of accountability, confession, and building relationships. Depending on the size of the total group, everyone counts off in such a way that small groups are created which consist of four or five women, including the small group leader.

The leader says, **"Now we'll divide into (__#__) small groups. We'll count off by __** *(2's, 3's, however many is appropriate)* **___ and I'll start...... One..."** *Everyone counts off.*

The leader says, **"The small groups will meet as follows: All the "1's" in Room ___, the "2's" in Room ___,"** *etc.* **"You're now dismissed to go to your small groups. Everyone please be back here for our group closing at (***time)* **_____."**

Activity during Groups:
Each breakout group should be led by someone with appropriate experience and sobriety. The small groups meet for one hour, dividing the time equally among the members (no more than 10 minutes per person) according to this outline:

Small Group Format:
Feelings check in (how you're feeling physically, emotionally, and spiritually)
Share accountability for "Bottom Lines"
Share accountability for "Top Lines"
Get current (share what's going on in your life)
Story time (a member shares part of her story or testimony – 10 minutes)
Prayer requests
Prayer

The whole group reconvenes for the Celebration of Sobriety and closing.

9. Celebration of Sobriety

After everyone is back together, members are encouraged to report their success and celebrate milestones of recovery. The L.I.F.E. Recovery Group recognizes significant periods of sobriety such as one week, one month, three months, six months, and one year or multiples of years. In addition to recovery "chips" or tokens, which are traditional in Alcoholics Anonymous, the group may provide some kind of memento, such as medallions or certificates, as recognition of these achievements.

The leader asks a group member to lead this celebration, and she says:
   "We believe it's affirming to recognize those women who are finding the L.I.F.E. of living in freedom everyday for significant periods of time. Is there anyone here

who's celebrating one week of sobriety? One month? Three months? Six months? A year? Or multiples of years?"

(Obviously, pause between each question to allow response. If a woman comes forward, present her chip, ask if she'd like a hug, and lead the group in applauding her. Those celebrating a year or multiple years of sobriety can be invited to make a few brief comments)

When those receiving sobriety chips have been recognized, the leader says:
"Is there anyone now who would like a "Surrender" chip to signify your willingness to surrender your acting out to Christ and live in sobriety for the next 24 hours?"

When all have been honored, the leader says:
"Congratulations on the chips you've earned and the chips you hold. We give God the glory!"

10. Closing Comments, Reading, and Prayer

Closing Comments:
The leader says:
"I thank everyone for coming and remind you the next meeting is *(time)*_____. We have schedules of other area L.I.F.E. meetings, as well as phone lists of group members willing to receive calls. If anyone has any unfinished individual business, you're encouraged to talk with your sponsor or accountability group this week.

    <u>**Please remember that individual anonymity provides the safety for us to risk exposing our secrets to others and to God's transforming light. Who you saw here and what was said here, let it stay here.**</u> **"**

Reading:
The leader says, **"I've asked *(name)*_____to conclude our meeting by reading 'The Hope.'"** *(Appointed person reads material.)*

Prayer:
L.I.F.E. Recovery Group starts each meeting with prayer, again usually the Lord's Prayer or Serenity Prayer, at the leader's discretion. The leader should then adjourn the formal meeting on schedule, but invite interested women to remain for prayer or fellowship among themselves.

Suggested Time Guidelines for Meeting

The timeline for a standard meeting of approximately two hours looks like this:

Welcome, opening prayer, and introductions	5 minutes
Welcome new members	2 minutes
Share readings	8 minutes
Offering and business discussion	5 minutes
Principle presentation and discussion	20 minutes
(Time to break into small groups)	5 minutes
Small Groups	60 minutes
(Time to return to big group)	5 minutes
Celebration of Sobriety	5 minutes
Reconvene and closing	5 minutes
TOTAL MEETING TIME	*2 hours*

L.I.F.E. Recovery Group Safety Guidelines

It is absolutely essential that every L.I.F.E. Recovery Group be safe. Safety produces the best environment for honesty and fellowship. All group members are responsible for observing these Safety Guidelines, and if they are violated, group members must confront each other in love. If an individual cannot observe the guidelines consistently or after being confronted, she will be asked to leave the meeting. The well-being of the entire group is more important than any individual member.

1. It is safe to be honest. We expect all members to tell the truth. However, in sharing, we avoid graphic sexual descriptions or sexually explicit language.

2. It is safe to have feelings. All feelings are acceptable to God and to us.

3. We will allow safe group conversation. We give each other feedback as long as it only reflects our own experience, strength, and hope. Therefore, we begin our feedback with "I," and not with "you." We do not give advice.

4. We do not preach. It is acceptable to share messages of spiritual strength and hope, to quote Scripture, or to make theological statements. We avoid comments that use words like "should," "always," or "never," and expressions such as "God says..." "God's will for your life is...," or "God will be angry if..." We all seek to follow Christ in our own way.

5. We do not shame ourselves or others. We do not put down ourselves or anyone else.

6. We do not blame anyone for our sinful behavior. We take total responsibility for our actions. Therefore, we keep our sharing focused on ourselves, not on others.

7. Contact between L.I.F.E. Recovery Group members via e-mail or phone should be limited to encouraging our sisters in their own individual recovery, or to promote the common good of L.I.F.E Recovery International. These contacts should not be used to solicit or promote personal interests.

8. We abide by the principle of group confidentiality. We do not reveal the identity of other group members or any other personal information outside the group, even to our spouses. There is only one exception to this rule. If anyone discloses feelings or actions that indicate she is a possible danger to herself or to others, including minor children, we will take all necessary action outside of the L.I.F.E. Recovery Group to report that danger and to ensure others' safety. Even more specifically, we must and will report to the proper authorities any disclosure of past or current unreported child or elder abuse, including possession of child pornography; and we cannot protect the confidentiality of illegal or "sex-offender" activity. <u>We are very clear about these exceptions to confidentiality</u>.

L.I.F.E. Recovery Group Covenant

To encourage a high level of trust, love, accountability and openness in my *L.I.F.E. Recovery Group*, in order to experience wholeness, healing, purity and freedom in Christ, I covenant with my group's other members to do the following:

I will make attendance at each group session *a priority*. During this time, I will choose the group first when making decisions about my priorities and time. I will arrive on time, knowing the meeting begins at_____. If I cannot attend, I will call my Group facilitator beforehand to notify them. This helps to hold me accountable in my attendance. I will commit my time each week to complete the appropriate unit of study in the *L.I.F.E. Recovery Guide before* the group session. I will confirm with my group facilitator that I have done the homework. This helps to hold me accountable to my recovery. Homework is an important part of recovery and we need to put time and effort into our recovery. Showing up and just 'drafting' off of the group is unfair not only to the group but to myself.

I will keep confidential all personal information group members share. I will not share matters from the group with any outside person or mention the information as a prayer concern. I understand that **what** I see and what I hear in this place **stays** here when I leave. I understand that breaking confidentiality could result in my being asked to leave the group. I may share with my spouse only those things I have learned about myself by being in the group environment.

I will commit to the following:

- To honesty, openness, a willingness to listen, and readiness to implement new behaviors.
- To reaching out and openly sharing my challenges instead of isolating.
- When I share, I will not be graphic or state names or places that were involved in my sinful behavior.
- To submit to the group to lovingly confront me when I am in denial or sin or am acting co-dependently in my marriage or other relationships.
- To support other group members in their desire to grow emotionally and spiritually.
- To be honest in my actions, thoughts, and emotions as I participate in the group.
- To be patient with other group members as we allow God to work in each of our lives.
- To not give advice or pressure other group members to do what I think is best.
- To inform my group facilitator of any physical or emotional problems that might arise through my participation in the group.
- To spend time with the Lord. This is time for me to hear from God and to get to know Him. This is time in prayer for me, and my loved ones.
- To journal faithfully as feelings and memories surface, for God has no time-line as He allows me to feel the emotions I have "stuffed." I know that whatever emotions come, God wants me to feel them. I give myself the grace to feel whatever comes.
- To surrender the changes that come to God, knowing that He will work this for my

good.   I also agree to surrender my marriage (all relationships) and my coping mechanisms to allow Him to make these necessary changes.   I understand I will need to do this daily.

I will seek to honor and observe the group rules.   This group is safe, therefore:

1. We can be honest.
2. We can be angry (even at God).
3. We can have conflict.
4. We can be sad, lonely or frightened.
5. We will not put ourselves or others down.
6. We will make no self-righteous statements.
7. We will not blame others; we will take responsibility for our own actions.
8. We will only give feedback when asked.
9. We will practice confidentiality.
10. We will strive to affirm ourselves and others.
11. We will pray for God's presence and guidance in all of our discussion.
12. Group time will be divided among those who have completed homework and ask for time to share. If unable to complete homework, we ask that you listen and not give input.

Please Initial: _____ I acknowledge that the **First Year of Recovery** and the **L.I.F.E. Recovery Model** (LRM) have been explained to me and I understand my active role in recovery. I understand that **L.I.F.E. Recovery** must report or cause a report to be made and cannot keep silent on the grounds of confidentiality or privileged communication in the following areas: • When a disclosure indicates a group participant may cause harm to self. •

When a disclosure indicates that a group participant may pose a danger to others (Child abuse, Spouse abuse or Elder abuse).

I have read the above and agree to the articles of this **Covenant** for the L.I.F.E. Recovery Support Group.

Signed: _____ **Date:** _____

The Mission of L.I.F.E.

Ours is a fellowship of Christian women who have a sincere desire to abstain from sinful sexual and relational behavior and to present lives holy and pure before God. Many of us have been trapped in the vicious cycle of sexual addiction. Ours has been a life of sexual or relational fantasy, ritual, sexual sin, and despair. We have felt out of control. We identify with the words of Paul in Romans 7:19:

> *"I know that nothing good lives in me, that is, in my sinful nature. For I have the desire to do what is good, but I cannot carry it out. For what I do is <u>not</u> the good I want to do; no, the evil I do <u>not</u> want to do -- this I keep on doing. What a wretched [woman] I am!"*

We realize our sin has grown worse over time. We have been addicted to the high of our lust, our sexual activity, or our unholy relationships. We have not been able to stop despite the consequences, and we experience great shame.

Ours is a history of broken promises, violated vows, wounded families, lost jobs, physical pain, financial chaos, spiritual bankruptcy, and even potential death. All through our difficult personal histories, what we truly sought was love and nurturing. We've been angry because we felt unloved, and we throbbed with unmet needs. We've even been angry with God because He didn't take away our temptations, our pain, or our problems. We have been bored with ourselves, with life, and with others around us. We have substituted sex or an unholy relationship for love, thinking that the high of these affording pleasures would erase our true needs of communion with God, a relationship with Christ, and genuine connection with healthy others.

Many of us have promised, "This is the last time I'll act out," but it was not. Don't be discouraged. You are not alone. Those of us who have chosen to become honest about our pasts and our emotions are experiencing healing with the help of the Holy Spirit. Many of us have tried to recover through our own thinking and on our own. We've even tried to manipulate God's healing through constant prayer, Bible studies, and church attendance. We are finding that God will help us heal only if we are truly willing to submit to His will by keeping ourselves humble and accountable.

If you desire what we have and are willing to go to any lengths to get it, we invite you to join us in the fellowship of L.I.F.E. - Living In Freedom Everyday - with the help of our all loving and all powerful God, through His Son Jesus Christ.

Seven Principles for L.I.F.E.

Following are the principles we follow as a path for healing our sexual woundedness, sin, and addiction:

1. We admit that we have absolutely no control of our lives. Sexual sin has become unmanageable.

2. We believe in God, accept the grace offered through His Son Jesus Christ, and surrender our lives and our wills to Him on a daily basis.

3. We make a list of our sins and weaknesses and confess those to a person of spiritual authority.

4. We seek accountability and to build our character as children of God.

5. We explore the damage we have done, accept responsibility, and make amends for our wrongs.

6. In fellowship with others we develop honest, intimate relationships, where we celebrate our progress and continue to address our weaknesses.

7. As we live in sexual integrity, we carry the message of Christ's healing to those who still struggle, and we pursue a vision of God's purpose for our lives.

Seven "C's" of Transformation

For some of us it's easier to remember these Principles in the form of Seven "C's:"

1. Conceit is gone.

2. Control is surrendered.

3. Confession is made.

4. Character is changing.

5. Contrition is offered.

6. Consistency is established.

7. Communicating "the hope" is essential.

These principles are a guide on the journey of recovery and not the magical cure. If you're willing to surrender your old way of thinking and the your methods of medicating your pain, then you, too, can live in freedom everyday in sexual and relational purity.

Because we come from different Christian backgrounds and traditions, we do not endorse any particular church or denomination. We have no opinions concerning race, economic or educational background, politics, philosophy, or differences between people as long as they claim Jesus as their personal Savior.

What we share is a common desire to be totally honest about ourselves, about what we have done, about who we are and how we feel, and about our commitment to remain sexually and relationally pure. We define sexual purity as the ability to be sexual solely through the expression of emotional and spiritual intimacy in heterosexual marriage. We define relational purity as the ability to connect intimately with others in ways that bring honor to God and bring no dishonor to anyone.

If you sincerely and humbly share these desires, we welcome you in this fellowship of women who embrace L.I.F.E. - Living In Freedom Everyday.

The Hope of L.I.F.E.

If we are truly humble and broken,
If we have genuinely surrendered our lives to Christ,
If we have confessed the exact nature of our sins,
If we continue to grow in our relationship with the Lord,
If we desire to become women of purity and integrity,
If we continually seek to correct the sins of our past,
If we remain constantly in accountability with God and with others,
And if we search for ways to spread this message of hope,
Then we will experience these promises of transformation:

We will know that God loves us because He created us as His daughters,
    and sent His son to die for our sins.
We will accept God's grace and forgive ourselves.
We will accept that there are others who love us regardless of who we are and
    what we have done.
We will stop equating sex or an unholy relationship with love and nurturing.
Our lust will diminish.
Our fear of being discovered in our sin will stop.
Our fear regarding money will cease.
Our anxiety regarding the future will fade.
We will learn how to make healthy choices.
We will become more in touch with all of our feelings.
We will heal from the wounds of our past.
We will be more intimate with our spouses and friends.
We will be better parents, adult children, workers, and women.
We will come to know, trust, and praise the Lord in ever increasing
    and meaningful ways.

Is this an unbelievable hope?
We think not.
Our lives are testimonies that God is working in us,
    Sometimes quickly and sometimes slowly,
    always toward His greater glory.

Definitions

Communication is essential to intimate fellowship. Fellowship is vital to L.I.F.E. - living in freedom everyday. Group discussions, feedback, and presentations are the life-blood of support and encouragement. Effective communication and fellowship require that we understand each other – that we speak the same language. Standard terminology is a tool for clear communication, and agreement about definitions allows each L.I.F.E. Recovery Group member to communicate easily with others in his own group and in the ministry network across the country. Each group member should study the following definitions to eliminate as much confusion as possible in regard to terminology. (These definitions may also provide a productive discussion topic for a L.I.F.E. Recovery Group meeting.) The definitions are based on my understanding gleaned from talking to hundreds of recovering people from a variety of geographic locations. Every group, though, may have local or personal understandings that are important in their setting. What's crucial is that the group discusses variations in meanings so that everyone can be clear about them.

90 Days

The term "Ninety Days" comes from the AA slogan "90 days, 90 meetings," which refers to the first three months of an alcoholic's recovery. Many times it's necessary for a person to go to a meeting every day for the first 90 days in order to remain sober. This commitment is a good one for all addicts, as well. In the beginning of your healing journey or after a relapse, committing to a "90 in 90" is an excellent plan.

Ninety days has also been applied to the period of time a sex addict may choose to be sexually abstinent with self and others, including his spouse. (You'll find more information about the concept of a ninety days' abstinence period in Principle Four, Assignment One.)

Abstinence

Abstinence is the act or practice of refraining from indulging an appetite or desire, especially for alcoholic drink or sexual intercourse; the state of restraint being without a substance, drug, as alcohol, heroin or behavior on which one is dependent.

Accountability Partner

This is any person who agrees to be in your network of people holding you accountable. A common mistake is thinking that you can have one accountability partner. I've never known a person to recover when he's only accountable to one person. One of your accountability partners can be your *sponsor,* but your spouse shouldn't be either your sponsor or an accountability partner. The word "partner" usually describes more mutuality in the relationship than is typical with a sponsor.

Acting Out/Acting In

Acting out refers to the practice of engaging in sinful, dysfunctional, coping, escaping or medicating behaviors. "Acting in" refers to rigidly controlling behaviors in an unhealthy way. It often means that a behavior is being strictly avoided, but the person isn't growing emotionally and spiritually. "Acting in" is often used synonymously to describe those anorexic with food or those who are sexually anorexic. "Acting In" also can be seen as an act of denial of appropriate self-care and nurturing, acts of deprivation that harm the care and value of self. "Acting out" and "acting in" are really opposite ends of the same continuum. They both can be attempts to control painful memories or emotions.

Addiction

Christopher J. Charleton, M.A., LCSW, is a specialist in the resolution of addictive and cross-addictive behaviors. Charleton is a member of The Society for the Advancement of Sexual Health (SASH), The International Association of Eating Disorder Professionals (IAEDP), and the National Association of Christians in Recovery, and the author of the book Relapse.

> Charleton states, ultimately, addiction means to **declare** that I am "**bound, devoted, or delivered over** to someone or something". (Online Etymological Dictionary, © Douglas Harper) Addictive behaviors, attitudes, and frames of reference which distort and fragment God's original design for us violate our sense of self. We betray ourselves by abandoning relationship with God and others for relationship with addictive substances and processes which culminate in isolation and estrangement. Addiction stems from painful ruptures and resultant betrayals associated with crucial life relationships.

Historically, the word "addiction" has been controversial in the Christian community. Some fear the concept of addiction removes personal responsibility for sinful behavior. Some believe those who call themselves addicts blame their personal decisions on an "addiction." All truly repentant and humble addicts, however, always accept personal responsibility for their actions.

The medical and psychological community has several universal criteria for determining if a substance or a behavior is an addiction:

1. **Use of the substance or behavior has become "unmanageable."** This means the addict has tried to stop, over and over again, but can't. There is a history of failed attempts. Some clinicians believe there must be a two-year history, at least, of an unmanageable pattern for a person to be labeled an addict. The word "powerless" has also been used to describe this pattern. Sometimes addicts refer to themselves as "out of control." Even when an addict creates destructive consequences for himself by sinful behavior, it's not enough to get him to stop.

2. **The addiction gets worse over time.** This means that more and more of the substance or behavior will be needed over time to achieve the same effect. An

alcoholic knows, for example, that as he continues to drink, he'll need more and more alcohol to get "high" or drunk. Sex addicts know that they need more and more sexual activity to achieve the same "high" of the acting out experience. This escalation can take two forms. The most basic is that the addict does more and more of the same kind of behavior. I've known, for example, people who start masturbating once a month and progress to once a day or more in the course of their addiction. For some addicts progression means they'll need new kinds of acting out experiences to achieve the same "high". It's important to remember that most addicts won't progress to illegal, highly dangerous, or sexually offending kinds of behavior. Some do, but the majority do not. Addicts may be able to stop their behaviors for periods of time, but until they find healing and the core issues driving their addiction, they will always return to them. Over time, a pattern of repeated failure will be evident.

3. **Tolerance is one reason for the factor of progression.** Medical science is discovering new things about the human brain that broaden our understanding of addictive behavior. The chemistry of the brain adjusts to whatever an addict puts into it. Over time the brain demands more to achieve the same effect. For alcoholics and drug addicts, the brain adjusts to substance and requires more. Thinking about sex and engaging in sexual behavior requires that the brain produce the brain chemistry to achieve sexual response. New research is finding that the sexual chemistry of the brain can also become tolerant, which means more and more thought or activity is necessary to have the same brain chemistry effects — the feelings of arousal, excitement, and pleasure. In many ways, sex addicts are drug addicts, as well as any behavior that elevates or lowers the neurochemistry in the brain. Workaholics become dependent on the adrenaline rush of expectations and deadlines, as a result we become high on the drugs produced in our own brain.

4. **Because of the brain chemistry involved, addicts use the thoughts and behaviors that produce the neurochemical highs to either raise or lower their mood.** We say then that addicts "medicate" their feelings. If an addict is depressed, lonely or bored, they can think of exciting encounters, either remembered or imagined, and the arousal part of the response produces chemicals that raise his mood. If an addict is stressed, anxious or fearful, they will tend to think of the relationship or a romance quality of the encounter. These associated brain chemicals create a feeling of well-being and contentment that lowers their mood. Most addicts are capable of both kinds of thoughts, and, therefore, can both raise and lower their moods depending on their feelings at the moment.

5. **Finally, addicts act out despite negative consequences.** Addicts don't pay attention to negative consequences and are in what's commonly called "denial." They also usually "minimize" or "rationalize" their acting out, despite the consequences. Until an addict decides to surrender control of their fears that prevent getting help, they'll continue to act out. Addicts may also continue to act out because it's usually a slow and insidious form of suicide, instead of immediately deadly. They know at some level they're destroying their lives, but their depression prevents them from caring.

Addictive Condition

Alcohol is merely a substance. Same with marijuana, cocaine and food. Gambling is merely an activity. Same with work exercise and sex. The point is, these things do not *create* addicts. They are simply the activities and substances that addicts *use*. So when we speak of addiction, we must understand that our concern is not with these activities and substances but with something else, something that exists independent of these things. We can remove every substance and activity from the life of an addict, but nevertheless, he is still an addict.

In fact, sobriety is simply a voluntary abstinence from all activities and substances in the life of an addict that are used to perpetuate his addiction. Stop using, stop doing, and you are sober. This is a good start, but you have yet to be made well because, as we stated above, something else independent of the addictive behaviors remains. This something else is what we call the addictive condition.

The addictive condition consists of a whole host of issues. Neurochemical imbalances. Abuse. Abandonment. Arrested development. Fragmentation. An incapacity for emotional wholeness and intimacy both relational and spiritual. These are the things that create addicts. These issues predate our addictive behaviors, they exist independent of our addictive behaviors, and they serve to perpetuate our addictive behaviors. We can achieve sobriety from our addictive *behaviors*, but if we fail to address our addictive *condition* we cannot heal. *Christopher J. Charleton*

Bottom Line

A "bottom line" is a boundary that refers to the distinction between which behaviors are tolerable and which ones aren't. An addict may have a bottom line as to what behaviors are outside of their sobriety definition, such as not spending time with others who still engage in a particular behavior. A spouse may also have a definition about which behaviors would cause them to leave if they happened again. This kind of bottom line is sometimes referred to as a "line in the sand." "Bottom line" behaviors are those that if engaged in may jeopardize our recovery plan and ability to grow toward healthy intimate relationships. If someone is recovering from romance obsession one of their "bottom lines" may include not listening to romantic music or watching romantic movies because entertaining those thoughts or activities would set them up for failure. Perhaps a shopaholic would no longer carry credit or debit cards or spend time at a shopping mall. Similarly a workaholic's "bottom line" may require strict adherence to leaving the job after 8 hours even if work is left undone. Re-evaluate and update bottom lines frequently. Our success with bottom lines give us hope that we will, in time, reach our top lines. For more information on this process, see Top Line.

Boundaries

In simplest terms, boundaries are guidelines for safety. They define which behaviors should and shouldn't occur in relationships and in families. They **pro**scribe what behaviors should *not* be allowed, and when these boundaries are violated, that is "invasion." Boundaries also **pre**scribe what behaviors *should* happen. When these boundaries are violated (or not upheld, to describe it another way), then "abandonment" happens. Some people have non-existent or "loose" boundaries, which frequently causes them to be harmed in some way. Other people have too high or "rigid" boundaries. They won't allow themselves to be loved or nurtured. Many people don't know how to establish their own boundaries. They might be codependent. Other people don't know how to observe boundaries. They might be perpetrators of harm or abuse. Stating your boundaries is a way of asking for safety, which is a different practice from making "demands." A demand is a request for more immediate action, which may have more to do with fear and anger than it does with personal safety.

Boundaries are limits for our protection as well as for another. There are six domains listed below to identify types of boundaries. Physical and emotional boundaries are generally known and understood; however, we'll take a look at other boundary domains that may not be so well known.

1. **Physical boundaries** are defined as what I will allow others to <u>do to me</u> physically, i.e. touch, physical proximity, etc., usually a distance just outside the reach of the others with whom you interact; as well as what I will <u>do to others</u>, also relating to touch or proximity. Who will I allow inside this perimeter; under what circumstances, etc.? No one is entitled to "invade my space," nor do I allow myself to invade the space of others.

2. **Emotional boundary** is defined as my freedom to own and express my emotional response to others or events. Emotional expression is the result of how I perceive and interprets events. Emotions can act as an alarm system or an expression that the environment is safe, comfortable, joyous, etc. Emotions are semi-automatic in that they may occur without conscious thought, or I may consciously decide how I will respond. My emotional boundary allows me to own and openly express, or repress or tolerate others. I own my emotions, and I allow you to own your expressions. In this way, neither is emotionally abused by the other. No one is entitled to tell me what I ought, or ought not, to feel.

3. **Intellectual boundaries** define my right to possess and define what I know. My thinking is my thinking; erroneous, flawed as it may be, it is mine. Understanding a proper intellectual boundary is to recognize that I know and what I know, and that is OK. The best way to describe this definition is by an example: as a child/adolescent growing up I was continually told that I was stupid and would never amount to anything, was too dumb to learn anything. That is an example of the invasion of my intellectual boundary. Statements in this example, for some, are damaging to their intellectual development. To establish and maintain a healthy intellectual boundary is to protect what you know without invading the intellectual boundary of others. No one knows everything, but all know something.

4. **Spiritual boundaries** relate to a healthy sense of self. We relate to this domain as self-esteem. Spiritual boundaries, also, while not religion, involve religion in its expression. Remember, Jesus allowed the rich young ruler, to whom He offered the saving grace that he was seeking, to have his liberty to walk away (Luke18:18-23). While Jesus was saddened by his response, He did not pursue him. In many ways,

the previous boundaries have helped to define this boundary – to define who I am and who you are.

5. **Sexual boundaries** are the limits that we place on our thinking and acting out with regard to our sexuality. They also include the physical aspects regarding the manner in which we will allow others to behave toward us and the ways in which we will behave sexually toward others. This subject is addressed more fully in another L.I.F.E. Recovery Guide in this series.

6. **Social boundaries** govern our social interactions that demonstrate concern for others and engage in behaviors that build relationships with others. - Spiller

Codependency

"Codependency is the fallacy of trying to control interior feelings by controlling people, things, and events on the outside." *Love is a Choice, Drs. Hemfelt, Minirth and Meier*

"Codependency is an interactive style of behavior attempting to minimize the risk of abandonment and rejection. Its origin lies in the survival strategies of a child desperate to win the love, affection, and attention of its parents. When parents are overwhelmed with their own life-dominating pain (disabled or preoccupied with financial, health or other concerns), the child unwittingly becomes conditioned to not further "burden" the parent. To do so would risk the parent's wrath, leading to physical punishment or being shunned. Correspondingly, the child develops a survival strategy utilizing hypervigilance to safeguard against rejection. Consequently, the child begins to consciously or unconsciously suppress itself, denying its own needs and wants for the purpose of being loved and accepted. The problem, however, is that the child is not actively being loved by the parent. In order to facilitate a bond with the parent, the child operates under the delusion that being perfect or self-sufficient will guarantee the love and attachment it so desperately longs for. This formula utilized to procure love is driven by self-abandonment - the child has to give by not being "needy" in order to get. As the child employs this survival strategy in later life, it engages in relationships where there is no reciprocity. They become the wellspring of infinite giving which "sustains" the relationship. To let one's true needs or wants be known would risk relational destruction. Underlying such codependent gestures of love is a chronic sense of terror, emptiness, loneliness and resentment. Codependency masquerading as love can never accomplish Christ's purpose because it is driven by fear; more specifically, by the fear of abandonment. 1 John 4:18 says "Perfect love casts out all fear, in fear is great torment, and in fear love cannot be made perfect." Although codependent-based relationships appear to be the ultimate in Christ-like servanthood and marital bliss, in truth they are characterized by underlying misery, bitterness, resentment, and fear. If marriage and friendships necessitate gaining the love, approval and acceptance through the abandonment of oneself, then the relationship can only work to the degree that the codependent does not exist." *Christopher J. Charleton, Relapse.*

Codependency was first used in the Alcoholics Anonymous (AA) community to refer to anyone who was in relationship with an alcoholic. The assumption was that these individuals tolerated drinking, as evidenced by their remaining in the relationship. These individuals, then, were considered "dependent" on the alcoholic. And since the alcoholic is dependent on alcohol, these people are "codependent" on alcohol. These people (usually spouses) tolerate an alcoholic and his/her drinking behavior out of their fear of being alone. It's more important for the codependent to maintain the relationship than it is to confront drinking and the problems it creates. As understanding about addiction has broadened beyond alcoholism to sexual and other forms of compulsive behaviors, the term codependent has come to refer to anyone who tolerates problematic or addictive behavior.

From this basic definition, many have written about codependency and said that codependents abandon their own needs and attend to the needs of the addict. They are more interested in maintaining the approval and presence of the addict than they are in speaking the truth. This objective causes them to ignore their own needs and wants and sacrifice themselves. This sacrifice is out of their fears, not out of their strengths.

Codependents often "enable" the addict by making excuses for him or her and generally looking the other way. They also perform many of the tasks that an addict should be responsible for, which led many to term codependents "doers." Accordingly, all that codependents "do" may save addicts from consequences, which often earn codependents the title of "rescuers." Finally, since codependents *seem* selfless, some have called them (and they may see themselves as) "martyrs." Essentially, codependency is a fear and anxiety-based disorder in which the individual has an addiction to approval.

Please be aware that any labels, such as codependency or co-addiction, are used only for the purpose of identifying problems that need to be healed. We should always seek to use these terms in love and not in judgment. Some primary partners (spouses) soundly reject these labels as humiliating. They might say, "It's his or her problem, not mine." These spouses could benefit from exploring why they choose to stay in the relationship.

Co-Addiction

Co-addicts are people who are in a *primary* relationship (such as marriage) with an addict. "Co-addict" defines a relationship between two people, just as "aunt" and "niece" indicates a certain relationship. Co-addicts may or may not suffer from the symptoms of codependency. Some co-addicts may not be consciously aware of their partner's addiction. They may seem strong and self-assured, but this appearance, too, can be a disguise for insecurity.

Compartmentalizing

In James 4:8, the brother of Christ says that we can be "double-minded." This term means that various parts of our brain can be at war with each other, which is certainly true with addiction. Paul, in Romans 7, says that we don't always do what we want to do, and that we often do what we *don't* want to do. One reason for this failure can be due to our "compartmentalizing." We segregate off parts of ourselves and aren't "unified." Another word for this state is "dissociating," which is a clinical term for a defense mechanism that refers to trying not to think about (or even to be aware of) something that is painful. Addicts often compartmentalize their sinful behavior and then deny that it even exists in reality.

Core Wounds – Traumatology

Addictive behavior is widely understood to be an attempt to medicate the pain of some past trauma or relational wounding that has not been resolved. The original emotional damage thus becomes a core issue, and the fact that it remains unresolved becomes the often subconscious excuse for the relationally and spiritually destructive behavior. The behavioral controls we impose, emotionally and spiritually, on childhood traumas as we mature into adulthood often serve only to rationalize and entrench the addictive behavior. We numb the pain over and over, often with increasing levels of the pain-killing behavior just to maintain that numbness. Satan is always there to use and intensify that inability to identify and express emotions, and to further disable our ability to have relationship with those we care about or even with God Himself. This L.I.F.E. Guide can help you invite Christ into the painful emotions associated with your suffering, and identify those core wounds from the past. Jesus himself expressed emotions in very open and often strong ways: He was moved to tears in the Garden, and to righteous anger in clearing the money changers from the Temple. Many of us have not been taught how to process and express such feelings. In order to heal, we must be able to express emotions in a manner that is consistent and constructive, and to deal with those core wounds in a safe environment such as a L.I.F.E. Recovery support group, where real relationships are built—open, transparent and accountable.

Cross Talk

This reference simply means talking back and forth during meetings, the process of feedback. Some groups have struggled with this concept because certain members may talk too long, give too much advice, be too angry or judgmental, or simply be rude. People are encouraged at meetings to be good listeners and not to be amateur counselors. Members should always seek to be loving in their feedback. Members in L.I.F.E. Recovery Groups learn to express their feelings and process pain and as these skills are practiced confidence builds and they are applied in daily life outside group. L.I.F.E. Recovery Groups not only allow cross talk, but encourage this dialog. A safe group provides the best environment to learn healthy intimacy skills and is essential for effective recovery. See the Safety Guidelines in the Meeting Guide section.

Cruising

This term refers to any ritual behavior (described in Principle One, Assignment Two) designed to find a partner to act out with sexually or relationally. Cruising rituals may include dress, appearance, facial expressions, flirting, "hanging out" in certain places, or any variety of behaviors designed to find or attract a partner.

Cycle

A cycle is a predictable pattern where one thought or behavior leads to others that eventually lead back to the original thought or emotion. The addiction cycle is explained in Principle One, Assignment Two, and the recovery cycle is described in Principle Six, Assignment Two.

Denial

Simply put, denial is avoiding or "denying" reality. Fear of consequences, such as others' reactions or our own painful emotions, is the usual cause for avoiding the truth. Denial involves both direct lies and the avoidance of reality.

Entitlement

All addicts need to "excuse" their behaviors. They search for reasons why it's okay to act out. One of the main excuses is called "entitlement," which means that the addicts "deserve" to act out. Some addicts keep a balance sheet in their heads and feel that when they've done enough good behaviors, they're entitled to do some bad behaviors. Some addicts feel so unjustly treated in life (martyrs) that they believe it's only fair for them to get something for themselves. Anger and narcissism are usually behind the feeling of entitlement.

Family of Origin

Your family of origin generally refers to your immediate biological family: your parents and brothers and sisters. It can also mean any people who have lived with you under the same roof. Examples might include stepparents, uncles, aunts, grandparents and cousins, but "family of origin" can also indicate others who lived with you, even if they weren't biologically related to you.

Family Systems

Dr. Murray Bowen authored the Family Systems Theory. A core assumption in this theory is that an emotional system that evolved over several billion years governs all human relationship systems. Bowen posited that "transmission between family members appeared to be based on prolonged association." Bowen further purported that "there seems to be a link to the deep inclination of human beings to imitate one another". Bowen has done extensive study in the area of family-of-origin issues. He is responsible for developing many family-of-origin perspectives and theories. Bowen believed that "individuals could not be understood apart from their family." Bowen believed that "the degree of unresolved attachment, or indifference between parent and child influenced how well a person functioned throughout their life." Dr. Murray Bowen explains the family as a system:

> *A family is a system in which each member had a role to play and rules to respect. Members of the system are expected to respond to each other in a certain way*

according to their role, which is determined by relationship agreements. Within the boundaries of the system, patterns develop as certain family member's behavior is caused by and causes other family member's behaviors in predictable ways.

The family system is also known as Family-of-origin. Family-of-origin is the source for launching children into adult life with the attitudes, behaviors, and skills that facilitate success. Some family-of-origin systems equipped children to be healthy functioning adults and some family-of-origin systems arrested this development. Early influences operate to shape future behavior. The shaping process occurs through the following four vehicles: "(1) parent-child emotional relationship, (2) parental guidelines, (3) parental approaches to child development, and (4) behavior modeling." The family system often sets up an individual to be vulnerable to compulsive behavior, addictive behavior, and life controlling issues. It can even go so far in modeling this type of behavior that an individual ends up imitating well into adult life.

Fantasy

Fantasy is an attempt at trauma resolution, an escape from reality imagining an *"it will be better when..."* scenario to provide a different outcome. Fantasies are thoughts about anything in an imaginary way, any preoccupation or obsessive thought patterns about the experience of using your 'coping mechanism' to change your mood or gain a sense of control and relief from your unpleasant emotional distress. We develop a dependency or affection for our behavior because of the relief (albeit temporary) that we feel. Fantasy has also been referred to as "preoccupation" –being preoccupied with the comforting thoughts and imagining the relief of your distress.

Chris Charleton, an internationally-recognized addiction/trauma expert and author of the book, *Relapse*, states that:

> "Fantasy is an intellectual process utilized to escape the powerlessness and helplessness associated with unrelenting emotional, relational and spiritual pain. Examining the Carnes addiction model clearly demonstrates that shame is the direct result of unresolved trauma and is compounded by the addictive process. Every addictive relapse intensifies and reinforces the already-existing shame. Shame is the emotional, relational and spiritual equivalent of AIDS, wherein a person attacks his or her own being. At varying levels, shame leads us to detest our existence, inundating us with feelings of inferiority, inadequacy, incompetence and unworthiness which are inescapable. It directly opposes God's proclamation of our lovability and worth.
>
> As shame becomes further entrenched within our being, fantasy becomes a desperate, last-ditch attempt to remedy the conviction of our unloveability, worthlessness and rejectability. Fantasy therefore, like the phoenix, arises from the burning embers of self-contempt and hatred to create a distraction from the immensity of our inescapable pain. Hence fantasies are an illusory and ultimately ineffective mechanism devised to counter our convictions of unworthiness for relationship with God, others and ourselves. Healing from the addictive process necessitates identifying our fantasies to

illuminate and ultimately conquer the shame-based convictions that are robbing us of the victory that God desires for our lives."

First Year of Recovery

There are *non-negotiable* aspects for a successful "First Year of Recovery" that are detailed in the LRM (L.I.F.E. Recovery Model). Before a successful first year of recovery can be experienced one must intentionally develop disciplines that pursue wholeness. One of these disciplines is a commitment to maintaining a recovery plan. Intentionally following this plan works toward consistent application of multiple disciplines that result in healthy intimate relationships where we are safe to express feelings and to process pain. Frequent evaluations of a recovery plan in the first year are crucial for long term success, especially at times when fulfillment appears illusive. The First Year of Recovery and the LRM can be viewed in their entirety on our website http://www.freedomeveryday.org/lrm/index.php.

Fragmentation

"Fragmentation is frequently the result of trauma. When a person experiences extreme emotional wounding from any source, a portion of his or her identity is compartmentalized in an attempt to handle or repress the resultant pain. When such trauma is repeated, the fragmentation intensifies until one makes the determination: "It is no longer safe to be who I am." Consequently much of the original personality is lost, destroyed or buried in an attempt to avoid the pain. The precious, God-ordained, original "self" with its corresponding hopes, dreams, goals and authentic desires is no longer accessible to the conscious mind. In this fragmented state, part of a person begins to operate like a wounded child who is at war with the part that functions like a rational adult. This often causes one's behavior to become erratic and disjointed, leading to relational dysfunction and intra- as well as inter-personal problems.

God's design for us is exactly the opposite of this fragmentation process. His nature, manifest in the Trinity, is the perfect example of integration: Father, Son and Holy Spirit in one unified whole. Wounding and the associated fragmentation render us incapable of recognizing God's intention for integration, and even blind us to our own disintegration. Without this integration, relational intimacy with God, ourselves and others is impossible. Fragmentation ultimately develops strongholds of resistance to God's plan for intimacy and integration. Therefore the path to ultimate healing involves breaking down those strongholds through honest self-examination and the willingness to face and grieve the pain which resulted from the trauma which shattered the original self." *Christopher J. Charleton*

Gaming

Gaming can become addictive when used as a means to escape from dealing with life stresses. A neurochemical high is received associated with pursuit and reward especially when gaming with sexual and violent stimuli. Gaming or digital/electronic experiences may also include: interactive virtual sex (digital/electronic enhancement of sexual experience) and anime/hentai (sex cartoon) utilization.

Grooming

Grooming behaviors are those which seem innocent, but are intended to gain someone's trust and therefore to gain an opportunity to generally benefit from someone or for making sexual advances. Both sexual perpetrators and sexual addicts sometimes engage in grooming potential victims or sexual partners.

Intimacy

Intimacy described in the Bible is seen in the Hebrew word "yada," "to know" by experience: to learn, to perceive, to discern, to experience, to know and be known relationally. For intimate relationships to flourish, whether with man or God, we must feel safe to reveal ourselves without holding back or keeping secrets.

Intimacy Disorder

Intimacy disorder results from the core beliefs "I am a bad and worthless person," and "No one will like me as I am." These ideas are foundational to addicts and co-addicts. Those who suffer from either disorder believe that if they tell the truth or express their real emotions, other people won't like them or may even end up hating them and leaving. This fear often means that the people whom we're most afraid of losing, like our spouse, will be the one to whom we are less likely to tell the truth. Intimacy Disorder is a fear- and anxiety-based disorder: Fear that someone will leave us, and the anxiety that we'll be all alone.

Patrick Carnes, a renowned addiction recovery expert states that, "more than 87 percent of patients come from disengaged families — a family environment in which family members are detached, uninvolved, or emotionally absent. All compulsive and addictive behaviors are signs of significant intimacy disorder and the inability to get needs met in healthy ways." http://enrichmentjournal.ag.org/200504/200504_022_internet.cfm

L.I.F.E. Recovery Model (LRM)

The LRM is a compilation of "Best Practices" for addiction recovery from practitioners, group facilitators and those who have implemented these practices to successfully Live In Freedom Every day. L.I.F.E. Recovery is committed to continually provide and update the LRM with proven addiction recovery information from a biblical and clinical basis. The LRM was created out of compassion for persons seeking sexual addiction recovery in an ever increasing and diverse market of programs, materials and books of which most offer incomplete or misguided information. The purpose of the LRM is now to provide proven methods for general addiction as well as sexual addiction recovery that unite the recovery strategies of individuals, organizations and ministries to work together, worldwide. Individually, before a lifetime of recovery can be experienced one must develop disciplines that pursue wholeness. These disciplines are presented in the LRM, with particular emphasis on the initiatives begun in the First Year of Recovery. When these multiple disciplines are applied consistently they result in healthy intimate relationships where individuals are safe to express feelings and process pain. There is great hope for those who view this model and follow its practices. See our website to view the LRM in its entirety http://www.freedomeveryday.org/lrm/index.php.

Medicating/Pharmacological Management

Medicating refers to using a substance or behavior to alter mood. Some substances and behaviors can elevate "down" moods such as loneliness, depression or boredom; and some can depress (or lower) moods like anxiety, fear, or stress. Medicating has been called "pharmacological management" in that the person manipulates his own mood, becoming like a pharmacist of his own brain.

Minimizing

Similar to denial (and really a form of it) minimizing literally means attempting to make smaller what is really true. Typically, a person tries to minimize how his destructive behaviors affect himself and others.

Narcissism

This is a clinical term that is more commonly used to refer to self-centered behavior. Narcissus was a Greek figure who loved looking at his own reflection. "Narcissists" often congratulate themselves on their own accomplishments or give themselves a wide variety of compliments. They seem to be thinking only about themselves and not about others. Their own agenda is the most important. Narcissists often seem very grandiose and self-confident or self-assured, but they really are not. Instead, they are very insecure and concerned about others' approval. Usually, these people have been "narcissistically wounded" - that is, they've experienced life traumas that have damaged their sense of belonging and of being worthy. Narcissists actually lack self-confidence and are trying to bolster themselves.

Neurochemical

All activities of the brain are facilitated by the interaction of chemicals in the brain. What is sometimes called the electrical activity of the brain is based on chemistry, or "neurochemistry." Scientists have identified hundreds of chemicals involved in the process of "communication" among brain cells. Some people are born with genetic predispositions to having problems with the proper balance of these chemicals. Addictive and dysfunctional behavior can also alter the normal state of brain chemistry. Psychiatry is the medical science that seeks to understand the right balance and prescribe medications to correct such disorders.

Objectification

This literally means to view someone who is fully human as an object rather than a person. Sexually, objectification means to see someone as only a physical body and not as a person with a mind and soul. Objectifying is de-humanizing. When we objectify someone, it's easier to lust after that person as just a body to be desired.

Rationalization

This is an excuse or justification. Rationalizations are used to try to explain why something was or wasn't done.

Recovery Plan

A recovery plan is an intentional effort working toward consistent application of multiple disciplines that result in healthy intimate relationships where we are safe to express feelings and processing pain. Before a lifetime of recovery can be experienced one must develop disciplines that pursue wholeness, all of which are presented in the LRM (L.I.F.E. Recovery Model) which can be viewed in its entirety on our website http://www.freedomeveryday.org/lrm/index.php.

There are **non-negotiable** aspects for a successful "First Year of Recovery" that are detailed in the LRM. Frequent evaluations of a recovery plan are crucial for long term success, especially at times when fulfillment appears illusive.

Relapse

A relapse is a series of slips that reflect the crossing of emotional and spiritual boundaries. A relapse is an on-going violation of sobriety.

Sexual Anorexia

Like those who struggle with food anorexia inhibit their eating, sexual anorexics avoid sex. Other clinical terms are "inhibited sexual desire" or "disorder of sexual desire." Painful memories (conscious or unconscious) shut down sexual desire or availability. Anorexia is often about anger and/or anxiety. Sex addicts can be sexual with others and anorexic with their spouses. In these cases, guilt, shame, anxiety, or a variety of other factors shut them down sexually within their marriages.

Shame

One of the core beliefs of addicts is "I am a bad and worthless person," which is a shame-based conviction. Shame, though, isn't inherently bad. There can be "healthy shame," which we feel when we know we need God. "Unhealthy shame" occurs when a person's life experiences, like trauma, lead him to believe he doesn't deserve God's love.

In Hebrew, Shame [H954], or to be ashamed, is defined as the confusion, disgrace, embarrassment, dismay, or disappointment that things didn't turn out as expected. Utter defeat pervades the mood, disillusion and a broken spirit will follow.

If shame still exists it hinders full development in Christ. Shame comes from past circumstances and experiences that injure our value. Shame must be vigorously uprooted and we must grieve the "injury" to our value or we cannot grow into the vision (fullness of joy).

Slip

A slip is a one-time violation of sobriety in any form. "Slip is an acronym for "Short Lapse In Progress." A violation of sobriety remains a "short lapse" only if the person learns from it, repents, and grows in understanding as a result.

Sobriety

Most simply sobriety is abstinence from any substance or coping, escaping or medicating behavior with an understanding that deeper core wounds drive the behavior(s) as a means of dealing with core issues. Sobriety is the condition of not having any measurable levels or effects from mood-altering substances or behaviors.

Sobriety for Co-Addicts:

As L.I.F.E. Recovery continues to work with those who are in relationship with an addict, we have found that certain behaviors, or the absence of certain behaviors, indicate sobriety for co-addicts and they are listed below.

- No Controlling and Manipulative Behavior
- No Enabling
- No Snooping or Playing the "Detective"
- No Fantasy
- No Transference, Taking on the Addict's Recovery or Behaviors
- No Self-Medicating or Escaping Behavior
- No Surrender of Values or Self
- Appropriate Boundaries and Respect for the Boundaries of Others

Sponsor

A sponsor is the person who is your main accountability partner. The qualities of a sponsor are described in Principle Four, Assignment One. While you will need many people in your accountability group or network, there will be one person who takes charge and helps you direct the show. This person helps you plan your overall healing journey, including meeting attendance, phone calls, counseling, and spiritual direction. He will not necessarily do all of these things, but he'll help you monitor how you are doing in the program. You will need to "submit" to your sponsor's authority and to determine what consequences will be appropriate if you fail to honor your commitments to healing.

Top Line

A "Top Line" is a boundary or behavior that guides or protects our becoming all that God desires us to be. Top Line behaviors support our recovery plan and require taking responsibility for feelings, actions and especially for the protection of our value. For example, spending time with others who are safe and demonstrate, or are learning, healthy boundaries and healthy behaviors would be a Top Line. Top Line behaviors can look like goals or objectives. We might include L.I.F.E. Recovery Group and Christian fellowship as a Top Line as well as studying addiction recovery material or other elements listed in the L.I.F.E. Recovery Model which set us up for successful recovery, each of these could be considered a Top Line. For more information on this process, see Bottom Line.

Trauma

Injury whether physical, emotional, sexual or spiritual to the true value of a person bestowed upon him/her by God to one created in His image.

Trauma Bonding

This is one of the trauma reactions described in Principle One, Assignment Three. It's commonly used to refer to dysfunctional attachments and unhealthy relationships. To be trauma bonded means that two people are attracted to each other because of conscious and unconscious characteristics that remind them of people earlier in their lives who wounded them. The unconscious hope is that attaching to this kind of person will provide a new chance to heal the old wounds. Basically, the hope is that if you keep repeating old behaviors you'll eventually get it right. Sometimes trauma bonding occurs when one person hopes this time to be more in control, to reverse the roles, or to be the one with the power.

Trauma Model Approach to Recovery

The Trauma Model approach to recovery seeks to uncover and heal the core wounds, with the belief that healing will alleviate the craving for the use of a substance or the need to rely dependently upon any behavior for validation or worth.

Traumatology – Core Issues/Wounds

Addictive behavior is widely understood to be an attempt to medicate the pain of some past trauma or relational wounding that has not been resolved. The original emotional damage thus becomes a core issue, and the fact that it remains unresolved becomes the often subconscious excuse for the relationally and spiritually destructive behavior. The behavioral controls we impose, emotionally and spiritually, on childhood traumas as we mature into adulthood often serve only to rationalize and entrench the addictive behavior. We numb the pain over and over, often with increasing levels of the pain-killing behavior, just to maintain that numbness. Satan is always there to use and intensify that inability to identify and express emotions, and to further disable our ability to have relationship with those we care about or even with God Himself. The principles within this L.I.F.E. Recovery Guide can help you invite Christ into the painful emotions associated with your suffering, and identify those core issues from the past. Jesus himself expressed emotions in very open and often strong ways: He was moved to tears in the Garden, and to righteous anger in clearing the money changers from the Temple. Many of us have not been taught how to process and express such feelings. In order to heal, we must be able to express emotions in a manner that is consistent and constructive, and to deal with those core wounds in a safe environment such as a L.I.F.E. Recovery Group, where real relationships are built—open, transparent and accountable.

Trigger, General

There are two basic kinds of triggers in our program. Any stimulus that is seen, heard, felt, smelled, tasted, remembered, or fantasized about that creates emotional and spiritual feelings of anxiety, fear, loneliness, boredom, depression, or anger is a general trigger. Often, general triggers are also referred to as "emotional triggers."

Trigger, Sexual

It is generally assumed that the word trigger refers to the stimulation of inappropriate sexual desire or action. Any stimulus that is seen, heard, felt, smelled, tasted, remembered, or fantasized about that creates sexual desire or action (even if only in the brain) is a sexual trigger.

We're conscious of many possible sexual triggers, such as looking at pornography or an attractive person. Memories of past sexual experiences (sometimes referred to as euphoric recall) can trigger sexual thoughts. Music, such as a particular song, can have the same effect. Other triggers may be more unconscious. They can be based on life experiences that we don't always consciously remember. Certain words or actions, certain expressions or tones of voice, certain times of the year or events, certain music, and certain sexual behavior can all trigger emotions or reactions. One key to identifying a trigger is to discern if your emotional reaction seems out of proportion to the event that's taking place. When that happens, your unconscious memory may be taking you to old places in ways you don't always realize. Have you ever had someone say, "You're overreacting"? The reason behind your "overreaction" is probably some unconscious trigger.

A Final Word On Words

Words are words. Definitions and understandings change over the years. It's never a good idea to argue about definitions. They aren't something to live or die for. Words are simply tools to help us communicate. If there's a disagreement about some term, come to a group consensus and move forward.

In addition to these terms that we've defined, your group may encounter many others that we haven't included. Please contact L.I.F.E. Recovery with terms you'd like to know about, have a good definition for, or simply think should be included in future editions of this *L.I.F.E. Recovery Guide.*

PRINCIPLE ONE

We admit that we have absolutely no control of our lives. Sexual sin has become unmanageable.

Confronting Reality: I'm Shackled in My Own Prison

Congratulations! Despite long years of deceit, lies, denial, minimization, fears, shame, and manipulation, you have picked up this *L.I.F.E. Recovery Guide* or have come to a L.I.F.E. Recovery Group meeting. You have been wanting to, thinking that perhaps you should, pondering if it was the right thing. You have resisted, found excuses, wondered who would find out, and worried about the consequences of getting honest. You've thought that no one would really understand. You've either believed that you have done the worst things possible (things no one else has ever done) or you've thought your stuff is not so bad - that you really don't need to come to a meeting and admit you need help. Hear these words:

Welcome.

You're in the right place.

We're glad you're here.

Imagine what it must have been like for the Prodigal Son. He just wanted to be home. He didn't think he deserved to return to his earlier status as a son because his sins were so great. He hoped merely to be like one of his father's hired servants. Maybe you're like that: You're just glad to be alive and able to get to a meeting. You'd like to simply be quiet and belong. The Prodigal Son's father, however, rushed out to meet him and prepared a great feast. That is what it is like with God. We want to be "imitators of God, just like little children."

You probably feel like a Prodigal Daughter. And in the view of society (as well as the church), that's much worse than being a Prodigal Son. Only men are supposed to struggle with sexual sin. You can't believe other Christian women hide similar secrets. You're convinced you must be all alone. Like a fearful child, you expect to be ridiculed or shunned if you show up at a L.I.F.E. Recovery Group meeting. You imagine the meeting notice is actually a mistake and that no other women will be waiting.

Well, dear sister, your fears are unfounded. It may feel like you're a little girl who has just come on the bus or into the lunchroom or onto the playground and you're expecting to be rejected or at least ignored. Instead, we rush over to greet you! We've been where you've been. We understand your pain and your fears. We're glad you've come. We can't prepare a great feast, but we can go to coffee later.

Your first assignment is just to get honest. We know that the greatest enemy of sexual purity is silence. We also know how carefully you've guarded your sexual secrets. It's hard to imagine letting them out. There are demons in your mind telling you, "No! You can't talk about that. Someone will go running and screaming out of the room!" We encourage you to confront those demons. Those voices have kept you shackled in your pain for too long. We know, because we're on a similar journey of learning to live in freedom every day. We want you to tell us how bad it got and what it was like to feel powerless over your life. Chances are that others in your group have done some of the same things.

Though you feel like a Prodigal Daughter, there is nothing - certainly no sexual sin - that separates you from the love of God. No matter what you've thought or what you've done, it's time to come home to the heavenly Father who loves you and is longing for your freedom.

The assignment that you are about to undertake will take great courage. It will be a risk and a challenge. Don't turn back now. Keep putting one foot in front of the other and head for home. The freedom you'll experience is worth all it will take to get there.

Assignment One - Admitting Our True Condition

As women, it's especially hard for us to admit we're sexually addicted. The label is so horrible! We cringe at the very thought. We'd much rather think of ourselves as love or relationship addicts, which sounds less offensive. Maybe we realize we have a problem with pornography or we've been involved in affairs, but to admit, "I'm a sex addict" is simply too much.

I hope it will help you to learn that the term "sexual addiction" is an umbrella term that describes a wide variety of behaviors. Just like we refer to a woman as an "alcoholic" without differentiating whether she's dependent on wine, vodka, or champagne, we use the term "sex addict" to refer to any of the various presentations of addictive behavior. Try not to get hung up on the label or let it keep you from the important task of healing. As you'll ultimately come to understand through your work in this *L.I.F.E.* Recovery *Guide*, "sexual" addiction isn't even about sex at all. Instead, it's about a desperate search for love and acceptance. You can surely relate to that definition, right?

Sexual acting out in women typically is more relational than it often is with male sex addicts. That's one reason we usually think of ourselves as love or relationship addicts. The most common presentation of sex addiction in women is a pattern of affairs or relationships. Females, though, engage in a wide range of problematic sexual behaviors. More and more women are struggling with on-line pornography and other kinds of Internet sexual activity. I've described these categories extensively in my book *No Stones: Women Redeemed from Sexual Shame*. It might help you to refer there to Chapter 4 if you need a more detailed explanation of the different presentations.

As you look at the following categories, note the ones you have done and indicate when your involvement in this activity started, even if it was only once. Try to remember how many times you have done each of these behaviors. (You may have to estimate. No one remembers, for example, how many times she has masturbated.) State how often you routinely engage in these behaviors (once a day or more, once a week, and so on).

Understand that these aren't necessarily discrete categories - that is, behaviors may overlap or cross categories. This division is meant to help you identify your patterns of behaviors, not to provide a "diagnosis" of a certain flavor of sexual addiction.

Typical Presentations of Sexual Addiction in Women

Relationship addiction	**Began**	**How Often**
One relationship right after another (*never being without a man, or at least looking for a man*)	_____	_____
Intense, emotional involvements, with or without sex	_____	_____
Most significant relationships become sexual	_____	_____
Simultaneous relationships, with or without sex	_____	_____
Affairs *(sexual or non-sexual, long term with emotional involvement, short term and non-emotional, one night stands)*	_____	_____

Romance addiction	**Began**	**How Often**
Fantasizing about people or relationships, real or imagined *(if married, these fantasies are not about your spouse)*	_____	_____
Fantasizing about sexual activities, real or imagined *(if married, may use fantasy to enhance sex with spouse)*	_____	_____
Intense, short-term relationships, with or without sex	_____	_____
Interested in the "chase," not in maintaining a relationship	_____	_____
Reading romance novels, including "Christian" ones	_____	_____

Pornography and/or cybersex addiction	**Began**	**How Often**
Viewing pornography (*Internet, magazines, videos, books*)	_____	_____
Participating in sexual chat rooms or sexting	_____	_____
E-mail or cybersex relationships	_____	_____
Engaging in cybersex activities	_____	_____

Stereotypical "sex" addiction	**Began**	**How Often**
Compulsive masturbation, with or without pornography	_____	_____
Exhibiting yourself *(even if "only" through provocative clothing)*	_____	_____
One-night stands or sexual activity with someone you've just met *(often alcohol use is a contributing factor)*	_____	_____
Visiting strip clubs or other voyeuristic activities	_____	_____
Bestiality	_____	_____
Sado-masochism (S&M) or pain exchange sexual activities	_____	_____

Partnering with another sex addict	**Began**	**How Often**
Choosing a sex addict for acting out partner *(there may be a fine line between sex addiction and co-sex addiction)*	_____	_____
Selling/buying/trading sex *(prostitution, stripping, using sex manipulatively to get what you want)*	_____	_____

Sexual anorexic	**Began**	**How Often**
Totally shut down sexually	_____	_____
Compulsively avoids sex	_____	_____

Writing Exercise: Your Sexual History

Plot a timeline of your life. One easy way is to draw a vertical line down the left side of a page (about an inch from the left of the paper), with your age marked to the left of the line at different intervals (beginning with your earliest years and continuing to your present age). This timeline, then, could be several pages long depending on the amount of history you have to record. In the space to the right of each age, record your <u>sexual and relationship behaviors</u>. (To accommodate the next exercise, leave some space after each notation in your sexual history.) The following questions can provide a beginning point, but add anything else relevant that comes to mind. One result of preparing this history is that you'll probably see how your sexual addiction developed over time.

1. What is your earliest memory of being sexual? How old were you? What happened? Was there anyone else involved?

2. Note the times when the frequency of certain sexual behaviors increased and when new forms of sexual acting out occurred.

3. Addicts act out when they are tired, lonely, angry, anxious, sad, afraid, or bored. Often these emotions work in combinations. Can you recognize times when these feelings prompted your acting out? If so, indicate on your timeline when this was true.

4. Every addict has made various promises and attempts to stop. List some of the times and actions you have taken to stop your sexual or relationship behaviors. Make sure to list your most recent efforts.

One of the clearest signs of an addiction is when we continue in a behavior even though we experience negative <u>consequences</u>. It's obvious to those around us that we're paying a high price for our behavior, yet we keep doing the same thing. What consequences have you experienced due to your sexual acting out? The next exercise guide you in plotting the results of your sexual and relational behavior.

Writing Exercise: Your Consequences

Make a list of your consequences and note when they occurred on your timeline. (Consider using a different color pen for your consequences.) Perhaps it will help you remember if you think of various categories:

Physical – Have you gotten pregnant when you didn't intend to? If so, what choice did you make about that pregnancy? Have you contracted any STDs? Or AIDs? Have you been sick in any way that is the result of the stress of your addiction? Do you experience any sexual dysfunctions (lack of desire, pain during intercourse)?

Financial – How much money have you spent? (Count the money you spent on clothes, grooming, and social activities that were part of your acting out.)

Social – Have you been divorced or lost a relationship? Is anyone really angry with you? Have you had to move from a certain place? Leave a team, club, or activity because of your sexual behavior? Has your sexual behavior caused problems with your parents or siblings? What about with your husband or children?

Vocational – Has your acting out affected your productivity at work? If so, has it cost you a promotion or some other career advancement? Have you lost a job or lost time at work? Are you underemployed or not able to work in the career of your choice?

Legal – Have you ever been arrested, spent time in jail, or been sued?

Some of you may turn to other resources to work through this material. Assignment One parallels the work of the Faithful and True Workbook, Unit 7: Lessons 1-3, and Unit 8: Lesson 1. You may also find similar inventories in the other workbooks listed in the resource section of this L.I.F.E. Recovery Guide. For this assignment you would include any work that you have done around Step One.

I applaud your courage in completing these writing exercises! You've done a tremendous amount of work. Don't worry if you realize you've left out some things. Outlining the truth about your experiences is an on-going process as you continue this journey. You've made a great start.

However, writing all of this information in your journal is a step toward being honest, but it is not the final step. The next crucial move is to share this information with others. I know that thought may be terrifying. But how long have you kept this information to yourself? Has it helped you to carry this burden alone? What lies have you told to cover up this story? It *is* a story, isn't it? It is a part of who you are. It doesn't define you, but it does belong to you. For years you've been thinking, "If people knew this part of my story, they would hate me and leave me. They wouldn't want to be around me."

Your feelings of fear have kept you hostage. They've been your oppressor. Your solitude of spirit has been the result. Silence has been your companion, and lies have guarded your silence. Loneliness has become all too familiar. You have had two lives: the one that others know, and the one that only you know. The public one may have many friends, but the silent one has none. Your silent self-pervades your existence and overwhelms all else in the darkness of your loneliness. It is time for your two selves to unite.

The only way to emerge from the darkness is to break the silence. That is what your L.I.F.E. Recovery Group is for. They are the sisters who will stand with you. They won't go running and screaming out of the room. They've probably done many of the same things you have. They will understand. Confront your fears. Be of good courage. Share the story. During a L.I.F.E. Recovery Group meeting you'll have the chance to tell your story to some safe sisters. (You may want to practice first with one or two members of the group.) You may not tell all of it the first time, but eventually you will. And you'll find tremendous relief in releasing the secrets.

(Please take note of this word of caution: **Don't be graphic in describing your sexual behaviors, especially not when sharing with your group***. You don't want to trigger other group members if you can avoid it. You also don't want to educate your sisters about other forms of sexual acting out.)*

Congratulations! You are beginning the journey of transformation into L.I.F.E. - Living In Freedom Everyday.

PRINCIPLE TWO

We believe in God, accept the grace offered through His Son Jesus Christ, and surrender our lives and our wills to Him on a daily basis.

Finding the Solution: I Have Only One Option

Assignment One – Exploring Our Reluctance

In the book of John, chapter 5, there is a great story of one of Jesus' healing miracles. As the account records, outside of Jerusalem is a pool called Bethesda, which was known as a place of healing. Occasionally an angel would come down and stir the water, and whoever got into the pool first was healed. One paralyzed man had been lying there for 38 years. (And you think you're worn out with your own lengthy struggle?)

When Jesus came on the scene and saw this paralyzed, despairing man, the Great Physician asked an unusual question. Now think for a moment. If you were the one who encountered this paralyzed man, what would you say? Perhaps something like, "That must be tough," or "How can I help you get into the pool?" You might be wondering about this man's condition.

Instead of one of those expected responses, Jesus asks a different question: *"Do you want to get well?"* To us, that sounds rather stupid. Why wouldn't a man who has been lying by a healing pool for 38 years want to get well?

But Jesus is the master psychologist. He knows what to ask to probe into the heart of our paralysis:

"Do you want to get well?"

It's a crucial question for recovering women today. Let's be honest. The Principles we're teaching you in this *L.I.F.E. Recovery Guide* aren't rocket science. The exercises and tasks aren't the least bit difficult to understand. Achieving sobriety and living in freedom everyday is a pretty simple concept. So why is it so difficult to do?

Answering that question requires that you examine your heart. Sure, a part of you wants to be free of your sin. In some ways you want to live in fidelity and purity. At least you'd like to be released from your shame. But do you *really* want to get well?

Writing Exercise: Do You Want to Get Well?

Write any reasons you can think of why you shouldn't give up your addiction. (Don't be pious and say you can't think of any.) What factors have kept you from embracing recovery? What excuses have you made about how hard it is to find help?

James, the brother of Christ, says that we can be guilty of being "double-minded." He writes, "Come near to God and he will come near to you. Wash your hands, you sinners, and purify your hearts, you double-minded" (James 4:8). There is a part of you that has wanted to get well and a part of you that has not. Sex or a relationship has been your most important need, and, as such, it's been an important "friend." It's been what you thought about in your loneliest and most stressful times. You wonder who and how you will be without your addiction. Your sexual fantasies brought you comfort, or so you thought. It's hard to think about being without them.

Understand that you may have to grieve the loss of your addiction in order to get well.

Yes, your addictive thoughts and behavior are sinful. That's true. But it's also true that you'll probably go through a grieving process as you take the journey of healing. It's a normal part of recovery. It's even necessary as you wrestle with surrender. God understands.

Luke 14: 25-33 talks about "counting the cost." That's an important exercise if you intend to be transformed. It's vital that you examine the depths of your heart – the reluctance as well as the willingness.

Writing Exercises: Counting the Cost

> 1. *Make a list of what it will cost you to get well. Which behaviors will you have to give up? (Review your work in Assignment One of Principle One if you need to.) Which friends must you avoid because they encourage your sinfulness instead of your purity? Will you have to change jobs or clubs or activities or residences? How you dress or where you go for recreation? The way you interact with the opposite (or same) sex? What on-going consequences are you going to have to face without acting out more? Be specific in counting the cost.*
>
> 2. *Next, examine your feelings. Write the emotions you experience when you think about what it would be like to be free from your sexual sin. Sure, you probably feel some gladness, but probe deeper. You also may feel some fear or sadness or even anger. After all, your addiction has been your friend for a long time. Confess to God all your feelings, the "bad" ones as well as the "acceptable" ones. Admit honestly to Him the parts of your spirit that may resist surrendering your addiction and your control over your life.*

Perhaps you're feeling ashamed or even hopeless after examining your acting out behaviors, the consequences you've experienced, and the part of your spirit that doesn't want to give up your addiction. You've remembered your earlier attempts to achieve sexual purity, and you wonder how this time can be different. What's going to make this effort succeed?

Your work in Assignment One of the first Principle highlighted your powerlessness over the sexual sin in your life, and you now see the depth of your bondage. Maybe you're more afraid than you've ever been. It's beginning to dawn on you that God, also, is aware of your sins. He knows the depravity of your thoughts and actions. How could there possibly be any hope for one like you?

This central question brings us to the heart of Principle Two. It is, indeed, a heart question, as you seek to repair (or perhaps to create for the first time) your relationship with God. Can you trust Him with your heart? Can you believe in the grace of His Son to be sufficient to cover all your sins? You're convinced your sin matters to God, but does your pain matter, too?

Despite our claim to be a Christian, when we're totally honest, most of us don't fully trust God. Many of us hardly trust Him. Some of us don't trust Him at all. You know you *believe* in God. That's not the question. The problem isn't belief; it's *faith*. **Do you trust that God will be enough?** That's the core question of Principle Two.

You may feel ashamed of this lack of faith in God. It may be one of your hidden secrets, along with the ones you admitted in your work of Principle One. You don't understand how you can distrust God, because you've been involved with religious things most (or all) your life.

The answer probably lies in the explanation of spiritual abuse. You may want to review the section in *No Stones: Women Redeemed from Sexual Shame* for a reminder of what it means to have been spiritually abused. Briefly, spiritual abuse occurs when someone uses the Bible more as a weapon than as a guide. It's when others attempt to motivate you into right actions by fear or shame, instead of by encouraging you into a loving relationship with God. Spiritual abuse also happens when you experience any other kind of abuse (physical, emotional, or sexual) at the hands of someone who is a spiritual figure in your life. That means that if you were abused by a pastor, youth leader, or someone in a similar role, you're automatically a victim of spiritual abuse.

Like other forms of abuse, spiritual abuse warps our view of God. We naturally form our view of God according to our experiences with our earthly parents, especially our fathers. If your dad was physically or sexually abusive, how can you believe God wants the best for you? If a spiritual authority figure was harsh and judgmental, how can you understand grace? How can you trust God to meet your needs and to love you unconditionally if you haven't known safe people who loved you, no matter what you did?

Writing Exercise: Examining Your View of God

Write a description of your view of God. What is God like in your mind? What are some words that describe Him? (If you'd prefer, draw a picture of how you see God.) Remember, the way you write or how well you draw doesn't matter. Don't worry about grammar or artistic ability. What's important is that you clearly identify what you really believe about God.

Most people who struggle with their sexual behavior feel terribly alone. You're isolated and desperately lonely. You feel alienated from God and others. Yes, the secret of your sexual sin keeps you from real intimacy with others, but the issue likely goes far beyond your problem with addiction. Your history of feeling isolated and alone probably dates back long before you started acting out. It probably began in your family. It comes from the core wounds of abandonment.

A thorough explanation of what it means to have been abandoned is found in primary sources like *No Stones: Women Redeemed From Sexual Shame*. I also give a brief description in this *L.I.F.E. Recovery Guide* in Assignment Three of Principle One. Review some of these materials if necessary.

For our purpose here, remember that we're abandoned when some of our fundamental needs for physical, emotional, sexual, or spiritual nurture aren't met by our caregivers. As I outlined about spiritual abuse in the last section, if a key spiritual figure in your life wasn't available in some way (physically or emotionally), then you've suffered spiritual abandonment. Again, that experience will color your view of God. You'll have difficulty believing God is really concerned about you.

Writing Exercises: Healing Your View of God

> 1. **List the people you feel abandoned you in some critical way. Describe the abandonment.**
>
> 2. **Find five Scriptures that describe God's care and concern for you. Write down the references. Read them daily for the next week.**

PRINCIPLE THREE

We make a list of our sins and weaknesses and confess those to a person of spiritual authority.

Telling the Truth: I Must Leave the Darkness

Assignment One – Admitting Our Darkness

Your earlier work in Principle One called for you to admit to yourself and your L.I.F.E. Recovery Group the truth about your sexual sin. In Principle Two you affirmed that God is trustworthy and faithful to transform your life if you surrender to Him. Principle Three confronts your sinful nature and eventually prompts you to confess your sins to others.

Working on Principle Three will be painful, just as it was painful to complete the exercises of Principle One. This kind of pain, actually, can be very helpful in the journey of transformation. Hurting reminds us of how far we are from God. The sting in our heart teaches us to turn to Him. Experiencing consequences forces us to let go of control. A tender conscience motivates us to refrain from causing more harm. Don't be afraid of the pain of these assignments, but instead, walk through it to the place of living in freedom everyday.

This third Principle challenges you to understand your dark side - your sinful nature. We are all sinners and fall short of the glory of God, according to Paul. We are inheritors of original sin: *the sin of pride.* Your addicted self – your sinful self – has pridefully (fearfully) tried to hide the truth about your life. You've believed that you are bad and worthless and that others wouldn't love you if they really knew you, especially if they knew about your sexual sins. You've feared that if people knew your secrets, they would hate you and leave you. These descriptions illustrate a principle known as **"intimacy disorder,"** which I'll discuss more toward the end of this assignment.

LIES: OUR WAY OF MANAGING OUR FEAR

The result of your fear about your sins' being discovered is that you've become a chronic liar. You've sought to manipulate the opinion of others, because you've feared being caught and facing the consequences. Perhaps you've arrogantly thought you could get away with your lies. Principle Three calls for you to courageously acknowledge the truth about your life.

Remember that we seek to admit our sinfulness not to increase our shame, but so that we can learn to depend more on God.

I hope you've already begun to tell the truth in your L.I.F.E. Recovery Group. I pray you've found it a safe place to share your reality and your pain. I trust you're getting some practice in exposing your darkness to the light. Allow God to illuminate the way as you work on these exercises.

Assignment One explores how you have lied to yourself and to others. Alcoholics Anonymous has many great slogans about recovery, two of which are applicable to our problem with lying. AA talks about an addict's "stinking thinking," and asserts "Your own best thinking is what got you here." Clinicians might say that we have "distorted cognitive thinking." Schools of counseling, both secular and Christian, sometimes approach our healing through attempting to change our thoughts. As Christians, we want to take every thought captive to Christ, including the stinking thinking of all the lies we have believed.

The first part of understanding the lies we've told to others is to understand the lies we have told *ourselves*. Lying is part of our original sin nature. When the serpent tempted Eve, he told the first lie, which was that she could eat the fruit of the forbidden tree and that she wouldn't die. Lying to ourselves often imitates that initial falsehood: We believe we can get away with something and that we won't get hurt by our sin.

Have you told yourself these kinds of lies? That your sexual sins wouldn't hurt anyone else or even yourself? That you were different, the rules didn't apply to you, and that you could escape the consequences? This stinking thinking is a lot like eating too much food and believing we won't get fat, drinking too much alcohol and thinking we won't harm our bodies, or avoiding healthy habits and assuming we won't get sick.

Did you ever convince yourself that you wouldn't get caught? Did you think you were being careful and discreet? What precautions have you taken to hide your secrets? What manipulations have you done to avoid exposure?

Did you assure yourself that your sins weren't so bad? Have you justified a "lesser" sexual sin because it prevented you from doing a more serious one? Did you believe that you had the power to quit acting out if you really wanted to? Did you tell yourself that your sins weren't all that deadly? For example, have thought that as long as your sins were never discovered, no one would get hurt?

Writing Exercises: Your Lying

- *What lies have you told yourself about your sins concerning your sexual and relationship behavior?*

- *Think back over your life. Do you remember the first lie you ever told to cover up sinful behavior? How old were you? Who did you lie to? Did you get away with it?*

- *Think next about the first lie you told specifically to cover up a sexual sin. Again, how old were you? Describe the situation and your lies about it. Did you get caught?*

- *If you can, trace the history of your deceitful behavior since that time. Make a list in your journal of all the major lies you've told.*

- *What was your most recent lie? When? Who did you tell it to? Are you still keeping it a secret?*

INTIMACY DISORDER: OUR FEAR OF BEING KNOWN

When we experience intimacy disorder, it is hardest to tell the truth to those whom we love the most. Another way of describing this phenomenon is that the person we are *most* afraid of losing will be the *hardest* one to let in on the truth.

You may be experiencing this dynamic in your group. It may have been relatively easy to come into your L.I.F.E. meeting and get honest. After all, the other women there are in the same boat. They, too, are sexual or relational sinners whose lives are (or were) out of control. You're reasonably certain you won't be judged too harshly, because the other group members have acted out in similar ways. And besides, the stakes aren't that high with your group. So what if they *do* think you're pretty awful? They're bound by a pledge of confidentiality and anonymity. They can't tell anyone else your secrets, and you can simply not return to the group. What have you lost?

You're finding it much more difficult; however, to tell the truth to somebody you really love. You may believe it's impossible to get totally honest with the most important people in your life. You're afraid you'll be stoned, which was the plan for the woman caught in adultery and brought to Jesus. Your fear of being rejected if you're intimately known is keeping you in bondage and shame.

Writing Exercise: Your Fear

Write the specific names of those people whom you are the most afraid of finding out the truth about your secrets, particularly your sexual sins. Next to each name, write the outcome that you most fear. Obviously, if you are married, your husband will probably be the first and most important person on this list.

Name	**What You Are Most Afraid Of**

How much have you been worrying about how others will react when they learn about your behaviors? Now, ask yourself if you're willing to go through life worrying about these kinds of consequences. Part of your process of transformation will be to build a character of honesty. You will no longer be comfortable living with your lies and deceptions. You'll long for integrity. Start thinking about the courage it will take to get honest with the people whom you love the most.

**One of the great principles of becoming faithful and true
is accepting the risk involved in telling the truth.**

Writing Exercise: Courage

Write a prayer asking for courage to tell the truth, even when you're afraid of the result. Ask God to help you trust Him with the outcome of this act of surrender.

Taking this kind of risk is one practical way we surrender our life to Christ. We clearly see that we can't control our own life. If we accept that God is in charge of our future, then what risks are we able to take? Other peoples' reactions, including our husbands,' are in the hands of God. Can you also surrender this outcome to Christ and dare to disclose the truth?

PRINCIPLE FOUR

We seek accountability and to build our character as children of God.

Growing in Transformation: I Mature in Character

Assignment One - Accepting Accountability

Principle Four is about accountability and about character. In the early days of learning about accountability you may have many mistaken notions of what it means. As addicts, most of us resist the idea of being accountable. We don't like being told what to do. We bristle at the thought of having to check in with someone. When an accountability partner gives or withholds her permission for us to do certain things, we protest that we're being treated like a child. We question why we should submit to another person or allow someone else to control us so tightly.

(Now, be honest: Isn't your reaction fairly similar to what I just described?)

This mindset is what makes most addicts resistant to the idea of accountability. It also represents many of the misconceptions about what it means to be accountable to someone about your recovery.

Let's examine first your need for accountability. You may still believe you can recover on your own. (Or maybe by now you're convinced of the benefit of being in a L.I.F.E. Recovery Group, but that's as far as you want to go.) I feel compelled to speak the truth to you in love: Remember, it's your *own* "best thinking" that got you in this mess, right? You thought you could figure it out on your own, that you could avoid the consequences, or that the rules didn't apply to you. These may have been some of the lies you told yourself. (Look back to the work you did in Assignment One of Principle Three.)

Here's what God says: "<u>Fools think they need no advice, but the wise listen to others</u>" (Proverbs 12:15, *New Living Bible*). A beginning point of accepting accountability is to recognize our "foolish" status regarding our sexual sins and our ability to change on our own. The wise woman listens to the advice of godly women who are further down the road in their journey of living with sexual integrity.

One helpful resource in changing your attitude is the book of Nehemiah, which gives a wonderful description of accountability. Chapter Ten of this *L.I.F.E. Recovery Guide* details the teachings from Nehemiah, and I suggest you read it as you work on Principle Four. The book covers a broad spectrum of principles that apply to the process of transformation, but many of them concern accountability. The first principle outlined from Nehemiah is especially applicable here: *Accountability begins with humility.* Admit your pride and your powerlessness to achieve lasting change on your own, and take another huge step of surrender. Become teachable.

Next, challenge your negative mindset about accountability. I encourage you to view the concept as a vital tool of recovery, instead of some kind of negative force hovering over you. Like boundaries, accountability provides guidance and protection for your journey. An accountability partner is someone who watches your back, who stays with you on the wall (refer to Nehemiah for an explanation of that phrase), and who walks beside you to steady you if you begin to fall.

This kind of primary accountability partner is called a **sponsor**, which is a term borrowed from the Twelve Step program of AA. This person is the <u>one main guide</u> who directs your program.

It's important to point out that a primary mistake made by recovering women is to have only one accountability partner. You may have tried that approach and it hasn't fully worked. As an addict, you're too smart and too skillful at deceit to let only one person truly know you. It will take more than that one woman to keep you honest and directed in the early days of your recovery. That's why it's so critical you participate in your L.I.F.E. Recovery Group and allow a *number* of women to know your heart.

But, as AA says, "First things first." In this initial assignment of Principle Four, you have one main job: to find a **sponsor**. Following are some descriptions of a sponsor to help you better understand what I mean.

Sponsors

And the things you have heard me say in the presence of many witnesses entrust to reliable [women] who will also be qualified to teach others. (2 Timothy 2:2 NIV)

These roles of a sponsor should be helpful in your recovery:

_____ A sponsor is someone who will hold you **Accountable**. With this person you will be able to share all of your past sexual sins, your acting out behaviors, your rituals, and your fantasies. Your sponsor will help you develop a plan for staying sober. If she ever sees you coming close to doing any of your rituals or acting out behaviors, she will directly confront you about them in love.

_____ A sponsor is someone who will give you **Encouragement**. As you slowly make progress a sponsor will celebrate your success. She'll be your biggest cheerleader.

_____ A sponsor is someone you can talk to and who will **Listen**. Whenever you feel tempted, lonely, hurt, frightened, sad, or angry, you can call a sponsor to talk thinks over.
Sometimes she will meet with you during such emergencies until the crisis passes.

____ A sponsor is someone with whom you can **Pray.** The two of you can seek the Lord's guidance together. You may also share Bible study.

____ A sponsor is a **Model**. Ideally, she should be someone who has had at least one year of sobriety from her addictions. Her success should serve as an inspiration to you.

____ A sponsor is a **Guide**. She'll teach you tools to use in recovery and show you the right path to be successful. She'll go over your *L.I.F.E. Recovery Guide* assignments as you do them. She can direct your reading outside of the group and may have ideas about therapy or spiritual direction. She is the general of your army.

Those descriptions are clearly positive, aren't they? They're appealing, rather than threatening. I think we all have longed for this kind of person in our lives. We can become interested in (and even welcome) an accountability relationship with this kind of sponsor.

Who, then, can serve as your sponsor? It cannot be your spouse, and it cannot be a member of the opposite sex. A sponsor should be someone you can relate to, and preferably someone who is a recovering sex addict with more sobriety than yourself. Some suggestions include:

- a relative	- someone in the church
- a friend	- someone in your L.I.F.E. Recovery Group
- a pastor	- someone with AA or SA experience

Some groups will be so new that there won't be women with lengthy sobriety. Fortunately, sponsors don't always need to be recovering specifically from sexual addiction, which helps combat the lack of recovering women to serve as sponsors. My first sponsor was a woman who had 10 years of sobriety from alcohol. Ironically, she didn't identify her own sexual addiction, which she was suffering from during her drinking days, until she had spent several years walking with me through my recovery from the disease. But she still was extremely helpful because she knew how to model accountability. Some L.I.F.E. Recovery Groups may need to rely on finding sponsors in other places in addition to just within the group itself.

In many ways having a sponsor will be like having a surrogate parent. A sponsor must be tough, wise, and loving. If you were abandoned emotionally, physically, or spiritually by one of your parents, having a sponsor may seem very strange. Addicts, after all, are impaired in terms of intimate relationships. We love to isolate and not be responsible to or connect genuinely with anyone else. On the other hand, a sponsor may also be a wonderful presence in your life that you've never found before. In the surrogate parent role, a sponsor can help heal some of your wounds from the past.

So just exactly how do you interact with a sponsor? What specifically do you do together?

Following is another checklist.

Concrete things you should do with your sponsor:

_____ **Call her every day**. (Yes, every single day.) If you're not in the habit of talking with her every day, you won't pick up the phone to call when you're tempted to act out. Ask your sponsor to check on you if you fail to contact her daily. Perhaps you only make a brief check-in to report that you're sober today and doing OK. Other times you'll need to talk more extensively about some situation or struggle you're facing. *Just be sure to make daily contact with your sponsor.* Talking by phone is better than sending an email.

_____ **Share how you're feeling with her**. During each daily phone call or email, report on what you're feeling. Identify if you're feeling glad, sad, mad, afraid, lonely, hurt, guilty, or ashamed. (You may be feeling one or all or some combination.) It's not your sponsor's job to fix your feelings, but it's good for you to get them out.

_____ **State any lustful thoughts or temptations you've felt during the day**. Remember, bringing the secrets into the light removes their power. As AA says, "We're as sick as our secrets."

_____ **Confess** any boundary violations you've committed or slips you've had.

_____ **Ask for specific accountability** about an area or issue as needed. As an example, you might ask your sponsor to question you about your computer use, or if you've avoided a former acting out partner when there's a possibility you might run into him. Maybe you need to ask for accountability about how you dress or where you go on your lunch break. You certainly need to be accountable about missing any L.I.F.E. Recovery Group meetings.

_____ **Process any circumstances or situations that are bothering you**. If you've had a fight with your husband or a friend, talk with your sponsor about what you could do differently next time. If you're frustrated with your boss, get your sponsor's input. *Talk about anything that is hindering your serenity.*

_____ **Work through these Principles of recovery**. Share your journal or notebook of the writing assignments in this *L.I.F.E. Guide*. Review especially your work in Principle Three – your "searching and fearless moral inventory," as AA calls it. The best way to do this work with your sponsor is face to face, if possible.

_____ **Celebrate your progress in recovery**. Be accountable about your sobriety date and celebrate milestones such as one week, one month, three months, six months, and a year. Take your sponsor out to lunch or for coffee and express your gratitude for the progress you're making with God's help and hers.

Summary of the Roles of Sponsor and Group Member

Useful in identifying, recruiting, and setting expectations with your sponsor

Sponsor Responsibilities	Group Member Responsibilities
Lovingly confront when needed, including possibly enforcing boundaries and consequences for group member	Submit to authority
Encourage the member with positive affirmations	Receive encouragement
Ensure group member submits a plan for her recovery and a contract about the sponsoring relationship	Prepare a plan of recovery and sign a contract with sponsor (see example)
Listen well (don't try to fix)	Share openly and honestly
Available to group member	Contact sponsor regularly and consistently
Pray with group member and teach her to pray more deeply	Pray on the phone and in person with sponsor
Meet physically with the member at least once a week and check the *L.I.F.E. Recovery Guide* assignments	Meet with the sponsor and show her the *L.I.F.E. Recovery Guide* assignments
Call the member if she doesn't call by a set time	Call the sponsor by a set time determined by the two of you
Strongly recommend the group member enters counseling if needed	Get a counselor if financially able
Ask the group member to state feelings	State feelings (use a feelings chart if necessary)
Ask if there are any lustful thoughts or temptations	Communicate honestly about the struggles of the day
Monitor the group member's self-care in terms of rest, diet, exercise, and living a balanced life	Practice healthy self-care regarding rest, diet, exercise, and balance between family, work and play

A sponsor can't meet all your needs herself, and she won't be perfect or 100% available.

<u>Only God can be trusted to be totally dependable.</u>

But a sponsor is a vital touchstone of your recovery program.

Writing Exercises – Accepting Accountability

1. *Is there anyone in your life right now who would be a candidate for a sponsor? <u>List the names of as many possibilities as you can think of</u>. Pray about each one and ask for God's guidance in your selection.*

2. *<u>Write down the date of your next L.I.F.E. Recovery Group meeting</u>. At that time, approach someone about being your sponsor. If you don't know anyone, your group may assign someone who has volunteered to be a temporary sponsor until you find a more permanent one. Don't worry about the temporary status. Just proceed in calling her every day until the next meeting and then try again.*

3. *<u>Write down the name of your sponsor</u>, whether she's temporary or a more permanent choice. If you haven't found one, note again the date of the next meeting and repeat the process of asking for a sponsor. If you're still not successful, broaden your search to something like an AA group, where there is usually more long-term sobriety.*

4. *<u>Complete the Sponsor-Group Member Contract</u> (sample given) to formalize the commitments you and your sponsor are making.*

5. *<u>In your journal, keep a log of the times you've called your sponsor and the times you've met</u>. Keep it separately from your other work so you can access it easily.*

The next four pages contain a "Sponsor Contract," which you and your sponsor should complete. The contract also has some sample questions and other criteria to help both of you understand and remain accountable to these commitments.

SPONSOR – GROUP MEMBER CONTRACT

Member Name: _____

Phone #s: *Home*_____; *Work*_____; *Cell* _____

Sponsor Name: _____

Phone #s: *Home*_____; *Work*_____; *Cell* _____

Group Leader Name: _____

Phone #s: *Home*_____; *Work*_____; *Cell* _____

Calling Schedule: _____ Sun   _____ Mon   _____Tues

_____ Wed   _____ Thurs   _____ Fri   _____ Sat

Format for Daily Contact: * *Details follow for each item*

- **Feelings Check** (share core emotions; not just thoughts)
- **Get Current** (temptations, boundary violations, bothersome thoughts or situations, etc.)
- **Accountability** (about top line behaviors and bottom line behaviors – see explanation)
- **Share Bible reading** or some other devotional or inspirational material
- **Prayer**

Top Line Behaviors:

1. _____

2. _____

3. _____

4. _____

5. _____

Bottom Line Behaviors:

1. _____

2. _____

3. _____

4. _____

5. _____

Others in My Accountability Circle:

_____   _____

_____   _____

_____   _____

_____   _____

Group Member's Signature and Date   *Sponsor's Signature and Date*

Explanation of the Items that Make Up Daily Contact with Sponsor

Feelings Check:

There are only eight core feelings: *glad, sad, mad, lonely, hurt, fear, guilt, and shame.* It's also possible to feel *numb,* which would be a ninth category.

Obviously, you'll experience gradations of these feelings, like *ecstatic* at just becoming engaged or *pleased* with the weather (both are variations of glad). You can be feeling *anxious* about an upcoming test or meeting, or *terrified* because you've just been diagnosed with cancer (both are nuances of fear). Bottom line, though, all our emotions fall somewhere in one (or more) of these nine broad categories.

Often we share <u>thoughts</u> and describe them as <u>feelings</u>. For example, you might say, "I feel like you're not listening to me." That's a statement of opinion, not a feeling. The feeling would be, "I feel *hurt* when you don't listen to me" or "I feel *lonely* in this relationship and *angry* when you don't stop watching TV to listen to me." See the difference?

Sponsor's Questions: *"How are you feeling now? Have you had any other strong feelings today? What were they?"*

When you communicate with your sponsor, include a "feelings check." Simply state your feeling(s) <u>in that moment</u>. If you had a different feeling(s) that dominated the day, share that, too.

Getting Current:

To get current simply means to describe your day, including both the significant events and the bothersome ones. Getting current is providing a "laundry list" of what's happening in your life, especially anything that's eroding your serenity. It also includes disclosing any boundary violations you've committed.

Sponsor's Questions: *"What happened today? Anything that's bothering you? Did you violate any boundaries? What are you grateful for today?*

Accountability:

Remember, your sponsor is your main accountability partner. She's the primary person you invite to question you about your recovery program. Your accountability report should cover your *participation* in your "top line" behaviors (explained below) and your *avoidance* of your "bottom line" behaviors (also explained).

Defining Bottom Lines: *Twelve Step groups often use the term "bottom line behaviors" to describe conduct you need to <u>avoid</u>, such as these examples:*

objectify

view pornography or other stimulating material

flirt or use sexual humor

control self (in the sense of "white knuckling")

compulsively watch TV

compulsively shop, clean, or do
    any other secondary acting out behavior

fantasize

masturbate

control others

compulsively eat

compulsively exercise

engage in sexual sin
    with others

Defining Top Lines: *"Top line behaviors" describe healthy choices you make daily, such as the following:*

eating well

playing

exercising/caring for your body

connecting with safe people

journaling your activities, thoughts, and feelings

resting

praying

Reading the Bible or meditation

practicing gratitude

Sponsor's Questions about Accountability

- *Did you engage in any medicating behaviors today?*
- *Did you objectify anyone today?*
- *Did you fantasize?*
- *Have you masturbated?*
- *Have you been on any inappropriate Internet sites?*
- *Has there been any provocative behavior? Exhibitionism?*
- *How much TV have you watched?*
- *Have you taken care of yourself physically? How much sleep did you get last night?*
- *Are there any specific areas where you need accountability?*
- *Have you fully disclosed everything you need to?*

Sexual Abstinence Period

These concepts about being accountable to a sponsor are tools to help you maintain sobriety. Hopefully, by this point in your progression through this *L.I.F.E. Guide*, you've achieved some length of sobriety from inappropriate sexual behaviors.

Obviously, sexual sobriety begins when you stop acting out sexually. At first glance, this "sobriety" definition seems straightforward. We addicts, though, tend to justify whatever it is we want to do, and we prefer to operate within a wide margin of behaviors we choose to view as not acting out. Being committed to a program of rigorous honesty (as well as being willing to go to any lengths to get well) demands that we scrutinize all our actions. As women, we often act out in subtle ways through flirting, sexual chatting, fantasizing, or using pornography. We rationalize that these behaviors aren't acting out because they don't involve overt, physical activity.

A healthy recovery program with transformation as the goal requires a total, absolute abstinence period from all sexual activity and intentional sexual thoughts. Abstinence could be for any period of time, but I recommend at least 90 days.

Neurochemical Benefits

An abstinence period serves several purposes and has a variety of benefits. First, by abstaining from sexual activity and fantasy, you'll experience a cleansing of your brain chemistry. Just like an alcoholic needs to be sober for a number of days before the alcohol is completely out of her system, the same principle applies to those recovering from sexual addiction. A sexual time-out is a form of detoxification. Remember, we addicts have a constant supply of our "drug," because even fantasies produce chemicals in the brain that cause us to feel pleasure. These chemical reactions are a natural part of life, but sex addicts have used this chemical reaction to medicate and escape their feelings. Stopping all sexual activity and sexualized thoughts allows the brain chemistry to return to normal.

Another benefit of abstinence deals with the addictive characteristic called tolerance. Tolerance means the addict requires more of the addictive agent to achieve the same result. An alcoholic, for example, develops tolerance so that she requires more alcohol to become intoxicated. In similar fashion, you may have built up a tolerance for sexual activity. You may find that you need a greater amount of sexual stimuli than you once did, which has led you into more frequent sexual activity or more dangerous sex. If you're married this tolerance factor may also have affected your ability to experience sexual pleasure with your husband. The need for more and more may even have created an inability to experience orgasm during marital sex. Being abstinent for a period of time will help to reverse these symptoms. After an abstinence period, you may find that the joy of sex with your spouse may return. If it doesn't, you may need more specialized counseling to unearth the sexual or (more likely) the relationship difficulty.

Correction of False Core Beliefs

An additional reason all addicts need to experience a fairly lengthy period of abstinence is for the purpose of changing your core beliefs. <u>We addicts hold the (unconscious) core belief that sex is our most important need</u>. Based on our history of sexual abuse or on the "false intimacy" we achieved through our sexual liaisons, we concluded that sex or a relationship was the way to get our needs met. Indeed, because we all are "needy" – the result of our abandonment trauma – we discovered sex was our most important need, for it was our best (though false) solution to the pain of our abandoned hearts. A period of abstinence exposes this core belief and gradually reverses it.

A period of abstinence will counteract another false core belief: <u>that sex is equal to love</u>. (Again, our trauma of abuse and abandonment created this lie.) If you're married, when you abstain from sex and still receive love from your husband, you eventually learn a new definition of love. If you're single, through abstinence you'll discover that you can find love from intimate friendships that you couldn't find in acting out sexually or through unhealthy relationships.

Suggested Boundaries for the Abstinence Period

You should observe specific boundaries during a 90-day timeout period to help you abstain from sexual activity and thought. Following are some suggestions:

- **No Internet use, except when necessary for work or to connect with your sponsor or support group.** If the Internet has been part of your addictive behavior, disconnect and lock up the computer for 90 days. (If your husband or someone else in your household needs Internet access, he can have the key). If the Internet is necessary for your work, discuss with your sponsor ways to avoid temptation. Using a filtered server or one of the accountability reporting programs are two ideas.

- **No alcohol.** Next to sex and relationships, drinking is one of the best ways to alter your mood. Don't drink.

- **No TV.** You may choose to make an exception for news shows, history or sporting channels, or similar appropriate fare, but avoid soap operas, talk shows, sit-coms and night-time dramas, which are full of sexual situations and unhealthy relationship examples.

- **Only G-rated movies or videos.** If you go to a family movie arrive after the movie previews.

- **Minimize fantasizing.** Many things can prompt a fantasy, but it's prudent to avoid those triggers that you know are problematic. As an example, music elicits powerful responses for many of us. If you're one who's strongly prompted by music, listen only to tapes or CD's, where you have control over what you hear. Review your list of acceptable music with your sponsor.

- **No reading of personal ads in newspapers or singles' publications.** Cancel any ads you've placed yourself.

- **No one-on-one conversations with men**, even "innocent" ones. You don't have to be rude, but do your best to avoid any personal exchange with men (or women if your acting out has been same-sex).

- **No objectifying.** Keep your eyes on the road, sidewalk, or whatever is in front of you. Attend to business and "bounce" your eyes away immediately if you see someone that triggers lust. (Another way to describe this suggestion is to avoid "public voyeurism.")

- **Change the routes you normally drive.** If certain roads bring you close to places that are triggers for you (e.g., where an affair partner lives or works) then choose another way to go.

- **Establish a defensive protocol when alone at home for 2 hours or more.** Call your sponsor or an accountability partner before or after extended periods of time alone in order to eliminate the "dead zones" of time when you're not accountable. Report what you'll be doing to stay out of trouble.

- **Connect with your husband or an intimate female friend every day.** Interact specifically each day on more than a superficial level. Share thoughts, feelings, and communicate concerns.

Withdrawal

Just as the alcoholic or drug addict goes through withdrawal when she stops using her drug of choice, the sex addict similarly experiences withdrawal symptoms when she stops acting out. Remember the neurochemical effects of compulsive sexual or relational behavior? The brain reacts when there is no longer that influx of chemicals, and that reaction may be noticeable.

Some addicts report genuine <u>physiological symptoms</u> of withdrawal including headaches, body pains, sleeping and eating difficulties, or gastrointestinal distress. All are stress-related reactions that may come from stopping the medication you've historically used. (These may also be symptoms of depression, which might be an underlying condition.)

It's important to remember that "this, too, will pass," as an AA slogan promises. You won't always feel so miserable physically. (I promise that no body parts will be harmed if you stop acting out. Orgasm is, indeed, optional, not necessary for life.) When you sense that familiar craving to act out, remind yourself that it's temporary and it will pass. Compare the craving sensations to running up a steep hill. The feelings will intensify and resisting will get harder, but if you choose not to give up and give in, you'll soon be over the crest of the hill and the going will be much easier.

Emotional reactions are another typical part of withdrawal. During abstinence intense feelings may surface - feelings you've kept bottled up for years. One principle of Alcoholics Anonymous is, "You can either drink or deal with your stuff. You can't do both." I believe the same standard applies to the sexual addict. Our sexual and relational behavior has been our way of "dealing with our stuff," and a sexual timeout often raises core issues that have been buried under the obvious symptoms of sexual sin. I predict you'll discover these foundational issues have little or nothing to do with sex. Instead, they probably involve your central woundedness and shame. An abstinence period allows you a chance to recognize and deal with these issues instead of medicating them through acting out.

Sexual Abstinence for the Married Woman

For the married sex addict, the issue of sobriety becomes more complicated. Certainly she must abstain from any extra-marital involvements, including those that are "only" emotional affairs. However, I believe it's vital for the married addict to observe the same total abstinence period as her single sisters, including a time-out from sexual activity with her husband. Because of neurochemistry, this abstinence period is important even if your acting out has involved "merely" pornography or masturbation.

Reasons for Marital Abstinence

In addition to the neurochemical benefit, the most obvious advantage of an abstinence contract for the married addict is to take the sexual pressure off the relationship. For many couples, marital sex has been full of conflicts, arguments, and emotional pain. Perhaps you've avoided sex with your husband and have preferred your acting out behaviors to connecting with him. In that case the pressure is from the absence of sex, but it's still pressure. Even if there's been little or no sexual activity in your marriage for a long time, you need to commit to an intentional period of abstinence. *There's a vast difference in deliberately choosing to abstain from sex and in avoiding it because of your addiction.*

Almost all sexual addicts (of either gender) are unable to be "present" during sexual activity, especially with their spouses. Instead of authentically making love with your husband, you likely are lost in fantasy about some other sexual experience, either real or imagined. You pretend you're with another partner or engaging in different sexual practices. You insist on darkening the room or you close your eyes to avoid being in the moment, because your fantasies are more pleasurable than what's happening right now. In effect, you're still having "addict" sex, even though the partner is your husband. Sexual addiction is an intimacy disorder, remember? Taking a break from marital sex gives you the chance to start over in your marriage relationship and learn to be present mentally, emotionally, and spiritually before you add sexual intimacy. Abstinence provides a chance to create *true* intimacy in your coupleship.

A bonus reason for abstinence is outlined by Paul in the following verse:

> *"Do not deprive each other except by mutual consent and for a time, so that you may devote yourselves to prayer. Then come together again so that Satan will not tempt you because of your lack of self-control."* (1 Corinthians 7:5)

Abstaining from sexual activity allows a couple to devote themselves to prayer and spiritual renewal. Time spent with God reminds us that our love relationship with God is our most important relationship and deserves first place in our lives.

Husbands' Response

To achieve the desired result in terms of your marriage, abstinence must be a mutual agreement that is very specific in its intent and plan. Never begin an abstinence period without prayerful discussion with your husband. (Getting help from a counselor may also be necessary, especially if your husband hasn't started to deal with his co-addiction.) In my experience, spouses' reactions divide into two basic categories:

• **Some spouses <u>welcome</u> a period of sexual abstinence**. Sex has been emotionally painful for years, either because too many demands have been placed on them, or the sexual activity has been unpleasant, or because the addict wasn't interested in marital sex. Whatever the case, a deliberate period of no sex is a welcome relief. These couples will have to work extra hard to overcome their intimacy disorder and connect on emotional and spiritual levels.

• **Some spouses, however, <u>fear</u> abstinence**. These husbands need the assurance of a sexual relationship. They worry that their sexually-addicted wives will continue to act out if sex isn't present in their relationship. They may suffer from the belief that if they were more attractive or performed better, their wives wouldn't have a problem. Obviously, as addicts, we know this belief isn't true. Our husbands' looks, sexual willingness, or sexual prowess aren't related to our sexual sin. For these couples, the abstinence contract teaches them to base their marital relationship on spiritual and emotional intimacy, not sexual.

A married couple should only attempt a period of abstinence if they also <u>have a plan for working on their relationship in other ways</u>. *Almost always, a couple needs to be in marriage counseling.* The intimacy disorder of sexual addiction is simply too deep and distressing for most couples to heal on their own. Issues of pain, betrayal, and mistrust will be paramount. Often other longstanding relationship problems will surface, as well, such as finances, parenting, household roles, etc. The wise couple will take their time and address each issue before considering a return to sexual activity, which can mask problems or create a false sense of resolution.

An addict/coaddict couple should <u>plan specifically</u> for their abstinence period. This blueprint might include a variety of strategies for developing healthy intimacy without relying on sex. Perhaps the couple goes to marriage counseling each week in addition to their individual L.I.F.E. Recovery Groups. Maybe they commit to working through the *L.I.F.E. Recovery Guide for Couples* or a similar resource to aid their healing. A wide range of marriage enrichment materials are available that could significantly bless your marriage. Take advantage of as many as possible during an abstinence period.

The following pages provide a sample abstinence contract for a married couple. Note that it has a place for a witnessing couple to sign. Meet with that couple, explain your goal and your plan for working on your relationship, and pray with them before asking them to sign your contract. Use this "sponsoring" couple for support and accountability as you go through the abstinence period.

Marital Sexual Abstinence Contract

We, _____ and _____, agree that we will be

sexually abstinent for _____ days beginning on _____.

We also agree that during this time we will do the following activities to increase our emotional and spiritual intimacy:

_____

_____

_____

_____

_____   _____
Husband's signature   Wife's signature

We have asked for support and prayer as we undertake this new step to increase the total intimacy in our coupleship. This covenant has been witnessed by a man and a woman who are important to our recovery and relationship:

_____   _____
Man's signature   Woman's signature

Principle Five

We explore the damage we have done, accept responsibility, and make amends for our wrongs.

Demonstrating Real Change: I Accept Responsibility

Principle Five marks a turning point in your journey of transformation. Here's a review of your work to this point as guided by the first four Principles: You admit the unmanageability of your life because of sexual sin and your inability to solve the problem on your own. Next, you choose to surrender totally to Christ and to seek God's will for your life on a daily basis. You inventory your history with complete honesty and reveal the truth through specific confession to another person. Then you address your flaws and inadequacies of character by entering into relationships of accountability.

These first four Principles are vital in forming the foundation for genuine, lasting change. You examine the depth of your sinful nature and your need for God. You take the huge steps of telling the truth and asking for help.

The journey this far, though, is also largely self-focused. These examinations and confessions and submission to accountability require great introspection. You're looking inward and exploring your own life, behavior, mind and heart.

Principle Five expands your investigation. It challenges you to look outside of yourself and consider the ways your sexual sin has impacted others. You admit that you're not isolated in your sin and that it has repercussions for others. People in your life are affected by your addiction. Your actions have caused pain for many, probably more than you'd like to think. In a variety of ways, your behavior and character flaws have harmed others. The process of Principle Five begins with a thorough assessment of the damage caused by your sexual sin, its consequences and your character flaws. Like Nehemiah, you venture outside yourself to survey the damage that exists in your environment. You observe the fallout of your life. You catalog the pain you've caused for others. You look unflinchingly at the harm you've brought about.

Assignment One: Assessing the Damage

It may be helpful to think about categories of harm. Examples include physical harm, emotional harm, spiritual harm, and financial harm. You might come up with additional ways your sin has hurt others. Prayerfully ask God to show you the truth about your actions and their results.

Remember the reason for exploring the damage: *It's not to increase your despair or add to your shame.* Be assured of this declaration of God's love for you, no matter what you've done:

> *"[The LORD] does not treat us as our sins deserve or repay us according to our iniquities. For as high as the heavens are above the earth, so great is his love for those who fear him; as far as the east is from the west, so far has he removed our transgressions from us."* (Psalm 103: 10-12)

The purpose of Principle Five is to grow in maturity as you move away from any denial, blame, or self-pity and learn to accept responsibility for your actions. As you consider the many ways you've harmed others, you gain a deeper understanding of how your sins have hurt the heart of God. The Prodigal Son (Luke 15: 11-20) provides a perfect example of a sinner who was willing to take full responsibility for his behavior. He understood, too, how his sin had hurt his heavenly Father as well as his earthly one.

Before you begin the writing assignments, read his story in the gospel of Luke.

NOTE: Consider this assignment a first step in identifying those you've harmed. It's not something you can compile one time and be done with it. As you grow in your transformation process, you'll identify others you should add to the list. Don't be discouraged if this assignment seems overwhelming or never-ending. It's actually a sign of progress when you become aware of the broader or deeper layers of pain you have caused.

Writing Exercises: Assessing the Damage

---

1. ***Identify categories of people you have harmed.*** Examples would include your current family (spouse and/or children), those in your family of origin, friends, coworkers, etc. Be sure to include those who've been indirectly harmed because of your addiction, such as spouses or children of acting out partners, or others who have looked up to you and been discouraged by your sexual sin.

2. ***List specifically all those you have damaged.*** Write each name. Review the categories of people in your life as a guide to help you remember each person. Start with those closest to you, like your spouse and your children.

3. ***Describe the nature of the damage next to each person's name.*** Again, be specific. Following are some concrete examples:

   - Broke the marriage vows you made to your husband
   - Missed important events with your children because of your acting out
   - Spent money on sexual sin
   - Performed poorly at work
   - Gave sexually transmitted diseases to others
   - Withheld intimacy from others (or was incapable of intimacy because of woundedness and sexual sin)
   - Acted hypocritically by violating your professed Christian standards

4. ***After the description of the injury you've caused each one, list your character problem that fueled the behavior,*** like your pride, selfishness, impatience, stubbornness, etc. (If you're not sure about the character defect, postpone this part of the assignment until you've completed Assignment Two of Principle Four, which deals with problems of character.)

Be sure to be gentle with yourself as you complete these lists. Talk about the process in your L.I.F.E. Recovery Group. Ask your sisters in recovery to remind you of your worth as a person created in the image of God. Your heavenly Father sent His Son to pay the penalty for the damage of your sin.

Principle Six

In fellowship with others we develop honest, intimate relationships, where we celebrate our progress and continue to address our weaknesses.

Living in Fellowship: I Cannot Succeed Alone

Congratulations on getting this far in your journey to maintain integrity in your sexual behavior and relationships. I know it's taken courage, perseverance and commitment. In many ways it may have been harder than you anticipated. You've experienced many feelings that may be new to you. You've had to humble yourself in admitting the full truth about your history, your thoughts and your offenses. But with God's help, you've done it. You've told your story of sexual sin. You've decided you want to get well and have surrendered your life to Christ. You've accepted accountability from a sponsor and perhaps have begun working with a counselor. You're willing to make amends to those you have harmed. I pray you're beginning to have a deeper sense of God's power and presence in your life.

Principle Six guides you into a way of living that involves genuine connection with others, instead of the isolation you've probably known. The foundation for this work comes from one of Mark Laaser's core teaching principles:

Fellowship is equal to freedom from lust.

It's probably hard for you to believe this promise. You may have been alone for years as you've hidden your sexual secrets from others. You've never known the joy of a supportive community. Your shame kept you from connecting with others, while it continued to fuel your lust and sexual sin. (You also probably can't imagine a life free from fantasy and lust, which have felt like your constant companions for as long as you can remember.) Principle Six offers a path out of your isolation, which in turn, is the road to sexual integrity.

Hopefully, you're already enjoying some of the benefits of fellowship through your L.I.F.E. group. You're bonding with other Christian women who've faced similar struggles and seek to live in sexual freedom and purity. You're beginning to experience both the grace of God and the grace of other Christians who will love you despite your mistakes.

Assignment One - Practicing the Program

Assignment One of Principle Six covers the basics of cementing this new way of life into daily practice. In this first lesson I'll actually be focusing on the *last* idea of the Principle itself: "We celebrate our progress and continue to address our weaknesses." I'll outline some specific, behavioral ways of walking the talk of transformation. **This assignment deals with the nuts and bolts of what the Twelve Steps community calls "practicing the program."** Developing true fellowship with others must be built on this foundation.

I'm sure you've become convinced that recovery doesn't just happen. Unless you actually do things differently, your behavior and attitudes won't change. Two slogans from Twelve Step language describe this reality: *"If nothing changes, nothing changes;"* and *"If you keep doing what you've always done, you'll keep getting what you've always gotten."*

Assignment One details a variety of specific ways to do things differently. I've already mentioned them as part of different discussions from other Principles, but it's important to outline them clearly here. Think of this list as a "paint by numbers" plan of recovery. By this point you consistently should be:

- Caring for yourself physically (adequate exercise, rest, healthy diet, etc.)

- Attending L.I.F.E. Recovery Group meetings

- Calling someone from your group every day

- Reading this workbook or some other helpful literature

- Enforcing healthy boundaries around your rituals and acting out behaviors

- Practicing honesty with yourself and others

- Taking responsibility for your actions

- Addressing your unhealthy attitudes and character defects

- Accepting accountability from your sponsor

- Participating in therapy if necessary

- Asking God's help for your journey each day

Obviously, you won't be doing each of these things perfectly every day, but this list is a blueprint of goals for your daily life. How are you doing?

The next two pages contain worksheets you can use as a daily inventory to measure your progress. <u>I suggest you make copies of these two pages and put them in your notebook or journal</u>. Each day, evaluate yourself in the five areas described and record your "Inventory Score" as indicated on the chart.

Exercise: Daily Inventory

Complete the Daily Inventory and record your score on the chart. Continue this practice each day for the next six weeks. Observe the pattern of your scores. Remember, the higher the score, the better. (Think about bowling, instead of golf.) Look at each of the five categories as well as your total score. Are your numbers increasing or decreasing over the days and weeks? If your scores don't show progress, you may be in danger of reverting to old behaviors and attitudes. If that's the case, perhaps you need to revisit the earlier Principles. Share your measurements with your sponsor and L.I.F.E. Recovery Group each week.

DAILY INVENTORY OF HEALTHY LIVING

Evaluate yourself daily in these five core areas using the scale shown below. The items listed are just suggestions; add others that might be appropriate for you. Give yourself an overall score for each area, then record those five scores on the Daily Inventory Chart.

0	**1**	**2**	**3**	**4**	**5**
Doing poorly		*Doing somewhere in-between*			*Doing very well*

PHYSICAL AREA	**BEHAVIORAL AREA**
nutritious eating	sobriety
adequate rest	attending meetings
exercise	calling sponsor/recovering friend
attending to medical needs	healthy work habits
recreation	financially responsible
physical self-care (brushing teeth, bathing)	enjoying a hobby
caring for possessions (living space, car)	avoiding substitutes for sex addiction like shopping, eating, drinking to excess
RELATIONAL AREA	**PERSONAL AREA**
connecting intimately with someone safe	serene, instead of depressed or anxious
considerate with spouse	receiving counseling
available to children	healing from core wounds
participating in supportive community	aware of feelings and needs
helping others who struggle with sexual sin	reading recovery literature
SPIRITUAL AREA	**DAILY SCORE**
prayer	**PHYSICAL AREA**
Bible study	**BEHAVIORAL AREA**
personal devotional time	**RELATIONAL AREA**
corporate worship	**PERSONAL AREA**
deepening spirituality	**SPIRITUAL AREA**

[Total score in each area should be between 0-5.]

DAILY INVENTORY CHART: WEEKLY

	SUN	MON	TUES	WED	THUR	FRI	SAT	**TOTAL**
Physical								
Behavioral								
Relational								
Personal								
Spiritual								
TOTAL								

[Total daily score will be between 0-25. Total weekly score will be between 0-175.]

DAILY INVENTORY CHART: SIX WEEKS

	Week 1	Week 2	Week 3	Week 4	Week 5	Week 6
Sunday						
Monday						
Tuesday						
Wednesday						
Thursday						
Friday						
Saturday						
WEEKLY TOTAL						

PRINCIPLE SEVEN

As we live in sexual integrity, we carry the message of Christ's healing to those who still struggle, and we pursue a vision of God's purpose for our lives.

Finding a Purpose: I Have a Vision

Assignment One - Telling Your Story

The first time you attempt this assignment you should have at least six weeks of sobriety. If you haven't been able to manage this length of time without acting out, go back to Principle One and Principle Four and work on them again. Here's a review of several things you need to think about if you're struggling to maintain solid sobriety:

1. Are you willing? Do you really want to get well? Is there still a part of you that's resisting the hard work that you need to do?

2. Have you really surrendered your life to Christ? If you haven't, get with a pastor or some other spiritual figure and talk about what's holding you back.

3. Have you confessed your sins totally? Have you really made a complete list of all your sinful sexual behaviors?

4. Have you truly put into place a comprehensive accountability group? Are you connecting with someone in the group on a daily basis?

Go over your answers with your L.I.F.E. Recovery Group or with several women who have long-term sobriety. Get some advice as to what AA calls the "next right thing."

This assignment is straightforward, but it will take some time. To tell your story may sound like a simple assignment, but it's far from easy. Assignment One prepares you to tell your story in the most effective way. You've probably heard a variety of testimonies in your life, like at church or at a meeting. Have you realized the best ones are relatively short? It's a greater skill to be succinct, which requires really thinking about what you're trying to say. You've also surely read a number of articles throughout your life. Are you aware the typical magazine article is in the neighborhood of only 500-1000 words? It also takes great skill to write briefly and to summarize your themes clearly and concisely.

For your work here, decide how you feel most comfortable relating your story to others. There are two ways to share your story, and the one you pick depends on your gifts and abilities. Do you like talking or speaking, or do you like writing? Which method is most comfortable for you?

More important than the method you use is what you include in telling your story. The tradition in AA is to share your "experience, strength, and hope" by sharing three things: ***"what it was like; what happened; and what it's like now."*** This simple outline is a great way to organize your story. Following are some suggestions about how to flesh out your account. You should include several aspects in each main division.

1. WHAT IT WAS LIKE

   a. *Your sexual history*. You can include any elements of trauma that you experienced, but try to keep this portion brief and generally descriptive, not detailed. You're trying to take responsibility for your own actions and not to blame others for the sexual sins you've done. Be specific about your acting out history, but don't be detailed or graphic. You obviously can summarize some behaviors by describing categories of acting out, like using pornography or masturbating compulsively or having affairs. (Don't mention the names of any affair partners.) Be specific about things like how much time and money you spent on your behaviors.

   b. *Your efforts to stop*. Describe your various attempts to stop acting out and make an assessment of why these efforts didn't work. Relate your emotional state during the frustrating times of not being able to find sobriety. Be honest about any level of spiritual or emotional immaturity that played a part in your failure to achieve sobriety.

   c. *Your consequences*. Outline the major consequences you experienced due to your addiction.

2. WHAT HAPPENED

   a. *Your "bottom."* When did you hit what AA calls your "bottom"? What happened that finally got your attention?

   b. *Your surrender*. Detail the day you really made a decision to surrender your life of sin and addiction. Go over any emotions and actions that were a part of this decision.

   c. *Your journey*. What has the journey of healing been like? What have been some of the significant moments?

3. WHAT IT'S LIKE NOW

*a. **Your current life.*** Describe how your life is different today than when you were acting out. What's changed? What improvements do you see? What have you learned about God, yourself, and the fellowship of Christ and others?

*b. **Your gratitude.*** Share your gratitude for God's grace, His transforming power, and what He's done and is doing in your life. Mention specifically the gifts you've found in recovery.

Writing Exercise: Telling Your Story

Prepare either a ten-minute talk or a 500-1000 word article relating the story of your sexual sin/addiction and journey of recovery. You can use any form of writing (long hand or computer) to write your story. You can prepare notes or an outline as if you were giving a talk, or you can actually record your story on audio or videotape as a way of practicing. You can also ask a safe friend to listen as you go over it.

When you've finished this preparation, report to your L.I.F.E. Recovery Group that you're ready to share your story.

PRINCIPLE ONE

We admit that we have absolutely no control of our lives. Sexual sin has become unmanageable.

Confronting Reality: I'm Shackled in My Own Prison

Congratulations! Despite long years of deceit, lies, denial, minimization, fears, shame, and manipulation, you have picked up this *L.I.F.E. Recovery Guide* or have come to a L.I.F.E. Recovery Group meeting. You have been wanting to, thinking that perhaps you should, pondering if it was the right thing. You have resisted, found excuses, wondered who would find out, and worried about the consequences of getting honest. You've thought that no one would really understand. You've either believed that you have done the worst things possible (things no one else has ever done) or you've thought your stuff is not so bad - that you really don't need to come to a meeting and admit you need help. Hear these words:

Welcome.

You're in the right place.

We're glad you're here.

Imagine what it must have been like for the Prodigal Son. He just wanted to be home. He didn't think he deserved to return to his earlier status as a son because his sins were so great. He hoped merely to be like one of his father's hired servants. Maybe you're like that: You're just glad to be alive and able to get to a meeting. You'd like to simply be quiet and belong. The Prodigal Son's father, however, rushed out to meet him and prepared a great feast. That is what it is like with God. We want to be "imitators of God, just like little children."

You probably feel like a Prodigal Daughter. And in the view of society (as well as the church), that's much worse than being a Prodigal Son. Only men are supposed to struggle with sexual sin. You can't believe other Christian women hide similar secrets. You're convinced you must be all alone. Like a fearful child, you expect to be ridiculed or shunned if you show up at a L.I.F.E. Recovery Group meeting. You imagine the meeting notice is actually a mistake and that no other women will be waiting.

Well, dear sister, your fears are unfounded. It may feel like you're a little girl who has just come on the bus or into the lunchroom or onto the playground and you're expecting to be rejected or at least ignored. Instead, we rush over to greet you! We've been where you've been. We understand your pain and your fears. We're glad you've come. We can't prepare a great feast, but we can go to coffee later.

Your first assignment is just to get honest. We know that the greatest enemy of sexual purity is silence. We also know how carefully you've guarded your sexual secrets. It's hard to imagine letting them out. There are demons in your mind telling you, "No! You can't talk about that. Someone will go running and screaming out of the room!" We encourage you to confront those demons. Those voices have kept you shackled in your pain for too long. We know, because we're on a similar journey of learning to live in freedom every day. We want you to tell us how bad it got and what it was like to feel powerless over your life. Chances are that others in your group have done some of the same things.

Though you feel like a Prodigal Daughter, there is nothing - certainly no sexual sin - that separates you from the love of God. No matter what you've thought or what you've done, it's time to come home to the heavenly Father who loves you and is longing for your freedom.

The assignment that you are about to undertake will take great courage. It will be a risk and a challenge. Don't turn back now. Keep putting one foot in front of the other and head for home. The freedom you'll experience is worth all it will take to get there.

Assignment Two - Understanding Our Cycle

In this assignment you will keep looking at that silent self that has kept you in bondage. The purpose of this assignment is to continue to bring into the light that which has been cloaked in darkness. It is also to show you some things that you will need to work on in a very specific and practical way.

his book *Out of the Shadows,* Dr. Patrick Carnes first described the predictable cycle that an addiction follows. I've also defined it in *No Stones: Women Redeemed From Sexual Shame.* You may want to check out those resources for thorough explanations of all the features of the cycle of addiction. Briefly outlined, it looks like this:

CARNES' CYCLE OF ADDICTION

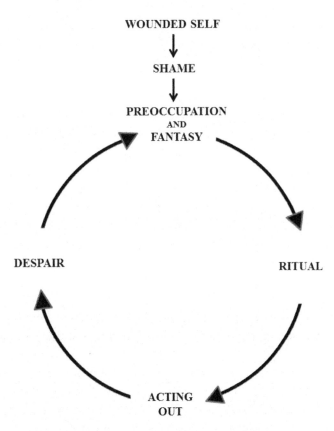

WOUNDED SELF

SHAME

PREOCCUPATION
AND
FANTASY

DESPAIR

RITUAL

ACTING
OUT

FANTASY is defined as those thoughts that you have about sex. It's also been referred to as "preoccupation" – you've been preoccupied with sexual thoughts and imaginings. The next lesson will help you understand more about your fantasies and what they mean.

Sexual thoughts lead to **RITUALS**, which are those things we use to prepare to act out. Any thought or behavior that you use to get from fantasy to acting out is part of your ritual. Most of your work in this assignment is geared to help you identify your personal rituals.

A ritual begins with **faulty thinking**, which launches the process long before you actually act out. The downward slide starts with the lies we tell ourselves. Alcoholics Anonymous (AA) calls these kinds of thoughts "stinking thinking." They come in different variations at different times. The following descriptions will help you pinpoint your own thoughts that lead you astray.

What have you told yourself about why it is OK to act out? As a Christian you've had to get around the fact that you're disobeying God's plan for sexual purity. Typically, we succumb to two main categories of stinking thinking:

Justification – For example, we might think that if we do enough good things for God, we're allowed to do a few bad things. It's like we have a balance in our heads - a formula we've worked out - and we reason, "God won't mind if I do these sexual things because I did so many other good things for Him."

The most obvious justification involves thinking about your spouse, "He doesn't understand me or take care of my needs. If he were just more emotionally available or more adventuresome sexually, I wouldn't need to do these things." Maybe some of us believe that being in a marriage will end all of our sexual lust. We think that if we just find Prince Charming, we won't struggle with temptation. We've read I Corinthians 7 about how Paul says that we should marry so that we don't "burn." When we find that's not the case with us, our faulty thinking tells us that our sexual struggles are our partner's fault or that we've married the wrong person. We then feel justified in committing sexual sins. We might even believe our acting out is a way we can satisfy ourselves so that we can tolerate remaining in our marriage. In our sick thinking, we see our sexual sin as having the positive benefit of preventing a divorce.

We also tell ourselves that it's OK to act out as long as "no one gets hurt." We think that if we can just keep our sin a secret, especially from our husbands, then no harm is done.

Entitlement – Sometimes we justify our sexual sins by thinking that we deserve it, which is a form of "entitlement." Many of us have said to ourselves, "Nobody loves me and no one will take care of me. I have to do it for myself." We believe no one else understands us and the pain we feel. Down deep we're angry about not getting our needs met, and we feel entitled to meet our needs ourselves, including using sex or unholy relationships.

Entitlement also tells us that we do so much, we work so hard, and we're so stressed that we deserve a reward. Because life is often so difficult, we might even think it's only fair to do these sexual things. We deserve some comfort and gratification.

Writing Exercises: Your Stinking Thinking

Complete these following sentences in your journal:

My thoughts of justification include ….

My thoughts of entitlement include ….

In addition to our faulty thinking, **painful emotions** also fuel our acting out. They, too, can spiral us into our rituals. Remember, acting out is usually an expression of our **anger**. We are lonely, yes, but it takes anger to get most of us past our moral and Christian beliefs.

Because of some of our painful experiences, both from our childhood, which we'll explore in a later lesson, and from more current interactions, we addicts are often very angry people. We're angry with those who hurt us. We're angry with those who failed to love us or meet our needs. We're angry with our spouses or former spouses. We're angry with those who have tried to confront us about our sins. In a nutshell, we're just plain angry. And we use that emotion to sidestep our commitment to purity.

Make a list of those people in your life that you feel anger toward. Next to each name, write down what you're so angry about. Remember that you may also be angry with God. King David, the "man after God's own heart," was furious with God at times, and he wrote many of the Psalms out of that anger. You also are probably angry with one other important person: *yourself*. Take as much time as you need to complete your list, and prayerfully ask God to help you. The following chart can serve as a guide.

Writing Exercise: Anger Inventory

Name   **Reason(s)**

_____   _____

_____   _____

_____   _____

_____   _____

_____   _____

RITUALS

As a reminder, we've been looking at our stinking thinking (justification and entitlement) and our anger because they're the beginning points of our rituals. Once we've justified our sexual sin somewhere in our mind, the next step is to prepare for acting out. These specific preparations are our **rituals**. It's important to identify our rituals, because stopping the ritual is key to stopping the acting out.

Following are some instructions to help you identify your rituals. You may want to make notes in your journal as you think through these questions. You may also need to talk to a woman from your L.I.F.E. Recovery Group to get insight into your rituals.

The best way to identify your ritual is to trace backward from your acting out behavior. First, select the sexually sinful behavior that you have done the most. Now remember the last time you did that behavior. What happened before you acted out? Back up in time to the point you first start thinking about acting out in that way. From that thought, what did you do next? And then? Those actions are part of your ritual.

If, for example, you've looked at Internet pornography, start by thinking of the last time you visited an inappropriate site. Retrace your steps to the moment you first started thinking about going online. Did you need to wait for private time, perhaps late at night or when no one else was home? Have you arranged for a confidential account? Do you have a secret screen name? All of those things are part of your ritual.

Rituals may be short, like the pornography ritual just described, or quite long. Some affair rituals take weeks or months to develop. They move from the first time you saw your affair partner, through initial conversations, to various acts of connecting before sex actually happened. Most people who have long term affairs cross many emotional and moral boundaries before they ever cross sexual ones.

There are as many rituals as there are individuals and forms of acting out. Some may be unique to you. Others are nearly universal. Some rituals may be quite subtle. For most women, how we dress and groom ourselves is often part of our rituals. How we flirt or touch people may also be ritualistic behavior. Carefully examine your actions with rigorous honesty.

Repeat this process of retracing your actions for any of your unholy sexual or relationship behaviors. Start with the most common ones first and then progress to the ones that you may have done only one time.

Use the chart on the next page as a guide to record your rituals. (To accommodate the next exercise, leave some space between each kind of acting out behavior.)

Writing Exercise: Your Rituals

Acting Out Behavior: **Ritual(s) Associated With It:**

_____   _____

_____   _____

_____   _____

_____   _____

_____   _____

_____   _____

Think and pray about how you were feeling going into your ritual. Were you lonely, stressed, frightened, angry, or anxious? This may take some hard thought and conversation with your sisters. Have you ever found that the excitement of just being in the ritual is enough to medicate the feeling? You may find that different kinds of sexual behaviors are associated with specific feelings. For example, you may find that feeling stressed or anxious leads you to acting out through pornography or cybersex, while loneliness leads you into connecting with an affair partner.

Writing Exercise: Feelings Behind Your Rituals

> *For every different kind of acting out behavior, write down (as best you can remember) how you were feeling when you started your ritual. Try using a different color to represent each emotion, like red for anger, blue for loneliness, etc.*

BOUNDARIES: The Key to Interrupting Your Rituals

One of the great challenges of healing and building a new life is to intervene on these preparations - the rituals – you've used to escalate from preoccupation to acting out. It's one thing to say that you want to stop a particular sin. It's more complicated to stop your ritual behavior.

It's almost impossible to stop the cycle at the acting out stage. You have to intervene before you ever get into your ritual.

A key principle to remember is that once your ritual has started, you will act out eventually.

It's imperative, then, that you create a plan to stop the ritual behavior. You must conceptualize what that plan will be – very specifically. You must outline the **boundaries** you'll need to keep you from entering into your ritual. These boundaries are the prohibitions which will keep you safe. They are the guardians of your sobriety.

Think back to a ritual that you described in the writing exercises. **What behaviors will you have to stop to avoid being in the ritual?** By identifying these behaviors, you can determine the boundaries you need.

For example, a woman who has had affairs must avoid the rituals that, in retrospect, propelled the connection to the point of acting out. Those behaviors may include one-to-one conversations with men, including phone conversations. She'll likely need to set boundaries about exchanging e-mails with men, going out to lunch, flirting or touching inappropriately, or maybe even being in places like bars or the health club where she might interact with men. These boundaries sound harsh and very restrictive, but in the early days of establishing sobriety, they're probably necessary. These prohibitions can be amended eventually as you get stronger in your recovery.

In another example, a woman who engages in Internet sexual activity will have to set boundaries to avoid the rituals that lead up to cybersex. Those might include installing a filter on the Internet service or putting the computer in a public place and using it only when others are present. She might ask someone else to maintain the computer password to ensure she'll adhere to the boundary.

For now, make a list of boundaries you'll need to put in place for each of your rituals.

Writing Exercise: Your Boundaries

Rituals: **Necessary boundaries:**

_____   _____

_____   _____

_____   _____

_____   _____

_____   _____

_____   _____

As I emphasized, rituals lead to **ACTING OUT**, which you've already identified in Assignment One. Are there any other forms of acting out you see you need to add to your list? If so, do that now.

The last stage in the cycle of addiction is **DESPAIR.** Another term for this desperate feeling is "depression." The vast majority of sex addicts are depressed. Go back and read the story of David for how he reacted to his own sexual sins. He was a desperate and depressed man. Pat Carnes discovered years ago that almost 75% of all sex addicts have contemplated suicide. Overwhelmed by guilt and shame, many women fear there is no other way to stop the pain.

Writing Exercise: Your Despair

Write or journal about the most depressing time of your life. What was that like? What were the circumstances during that time? Have you ever thought about suicide? Have you ever acted on those thoughts? Are you feeling suicidal now?

You may find that you need to be evaluated for clinical depression, which means that you see a professional to assess your level of despair. You might start with a counselor or therapist. If warranted, this clinician may refer you to a medical doctor, like a psychiatrist, who can map out a plan of treatment. (Some family practitioners, internists, or gynecologists will also address depression.) **If you feel suicidal at any time, it's vital you share those thoughts with a professional and get adequate help.**

ADDITIONAL WAYS OF ACTING OUT

Refer back to the cycle of addiction diagram and note that the point of despair leads back into preoccupation and fantasy. Sex addicts seek to relieve their feelings of despair. As crazy as it may seem, the best way to get relief is to start the process all over again. Addicts will return to the high of sexual fantasy and the cycle repeats.

For some of us, it's important to recognize that we also turn to other behaviors that medicate the feeling of despair. Roughly half of all sex addicts are alcoholics or chemically dependent. Many are smokers, hooked on caffeine, or on other "normal" drugs. Some turn to behaviors like work, sports, TV watching, or spending. We now know that many sex addicts are multiply addicted; i.e., they suffer from more than one addiction. It's common for many alcoholics, for example, to discover after they have months or years of recovery that they are also sex addicts. In the journey of your healing, you may need to deal with other substances or behaviors that you use to alter your moods.

For many women, especially those within the Christian community, one way we try to alter our mood is through religious service. We volunteer to visit the shut-ins or we organize the church bazaar. These are good activities, of course, but if we're excruciatingly honest, we know we're doing them primarily to avoid our feelings, instead of from pure motives. Or another favorite diversion tactic for women is to focus on their children. We pour ourselves into our kids' lives to avoid having to face our own. And then, of course, there's always shopping or eating. One of my personal favorites is cleaning. If I can't control my feelings, I can at least control dirt! The list of other medicating behaviors could be endless. It will take you a period of sobriety from sexual addiction to recognize some of the additional behaviors you use to deal with your despair.

Writing Exercise: Your Additional Behaviors

> *Based on your awareness now, make a list of other addictions or ways you use to medicate the pain of your acting out.*

After all this hard work, take a grace break. Remember that we are all sinners and stuck in the cycle of our own sinful thinking and behavior. Even Paul admitted that he *didn't* do the good things he wanted to do, and he *did* do the things that he didn't want to. He said, "Oh, what a wretched man am I!"

Do you think God sent his Son to earth because we were perfect? God simply asks you to lean on Him more and more each day, and one day at a time begin to understand how much he loves you. Remember again the story of the Prodigal Son and focus on how the father rushes out to meet his child. God is watching for you to come home, daughter, and he is preparing for a feast.

PRINCIPLE TWO

We believe in God, accept the grace offered through His Son Jesus Christ, and surrender our lives and our wills to Him on a daily basis.

Finding the Solution: I Have Only One Option

Assignment Two - Surrendering Control

A subtitle for Assignment Two could be "the choice I've never made." You may be feeling defensive after reading that heading. Maybe you bristle at the implication you haven't tried to do something about your addiction. You've probably done a lot of things about your addiction – except become sober from it.

Most of our attempts to deal with our addiction are unsuccessful because they're more about controlling our behavior or lust, instead of surrendering it. We use a variety of excuses to rationalize this approach. (Review Assignment Two of Principle One, which outlines several examples of this kind of "stinking thinking.") We also excuse half-hearted attempts to surrender with rationalizations like, "I don't want to make radical changes like ending a 'friendship' because that might embarrass my family when people question why;" or "God knows I need to support myself financially, so it's understandable that I can't quit traveling for my job."

In more subtle ways we sometimes try to control or bargain with God about our addiction. We make attempts to stop acting out, and bargain that God will do something for us in exchange. Some of you have heard my story about surrendering my involvement in affairs in exchange for God's making me a famous writer. As a young bride, I dedicated myself to "writing for God" and vowed to refrain from my pattern of sexual sin. In my spiritual immaturity, I believed God would reward me with literary success. I fantasized about winning the Pulitzer Prize and witnessing about my faith. If you had asked me, I'd have assured you I'd tried to surrender my habit to God. What I'd really done was attempt to manipulate God into giving me something I deeply wanted: to be an acclaimed author.

Most of us have made many of these surrogate surrenders. We're usually quick to "surrender" when we're facing tough consequences of our addiction. We're afraid we're pregnant, so we promise to stop the affair if God will only spare us the complication of pregnancy. Or we try to get by with a partial surrender. We give up an acting out behavior that we think is especially bad, but we hold on to other, supposedly less offensive, behaviors. We end an affair, but we continue to use pornography or masturbate. That approach is really only substituting one sin for another. That exchange hardly constitutes genuine surrender!

111

Sometimes we may even stop acting out totally for a while (by "white knuckling"), but we don't truly surrender our hearts and wills to God.

Some of us have tried to manipulate and control others, especially our spouses, by pseudo efforts to surrender. We may stop acting out with other people, but instead we bug our husband excessively for sex. We may agree to go to counseling as long as our mate agrees to stop pestering us about it. But though we sit in a counselor's office for an hour a week, we never commit to a genuine process of change.

Occasionally, an addict will surrender the specifics of her sexual addiction, but will continue to hold on to her heart. By that I mean that the now-sober addict will refuse to look any deeper than the sinful behaviors. If she's not physically acting out, she considers herself cured. She won't look at her character defects of pride or jealousy or insecurity or control. She's really nothing more than what AA calls a "dry drunk." Usually, she's still medicating with other more acceptable means like working or spending or losing herself in her children.

That kind of "surrender" falls far short of God's call. He challenges us to "offer your bodies as living sacrifices, holy and pleasing to God – this is your spiritual act of worship. Do not conform any longer to the pattern of this world, but be transformed by the renewing of your mind" (Romans 12: 1). *God is much more concerned with our transformation than with our mere sobriety.* Can you honestly say you've truly surrendered to God in a spiritual sense? Are you willing to allow Him to transform you and mold you into the person He wants you to be?

A final example of a false kind of "choice" we make to surrender is our attempt to get sober on our own. Because of our shame and our fear of being known, we're tempted to try to recover without involving anyone else in our process. We believe we can recover in isolation by simply reading books, completing workbook exercises, or maybe talking with a therapist. But we won't share with other women individually, and we sure won't go to a group where others are seeking to become sexually and relationally pure.

This persistence of seeking recovery without becoming vulnerable to others exposes a key stronghold in many addicts' lives: the belief "I can do this on my own!" *We trust our ability to help ourselves more than we trust God.* We hope that if we just try long enough, hard enough, or "right" enough, we'll be successful. Instead of admitting powerlessness and surrendering totally to God, we try to work harder at getting it right by ourselves. Such efforts are doomed to fail. (I'll talk more in a later Principle about the pitfalls of refusing to be in accountability and fellowship with others.)

Writing Exercises: Reviewing Your Choices

1. *What are your excuses for not surrendering your addiction totally to God?*

2. *List some of the deals you've made with God about your acting out.*

3. *How have you tried to control or manipulate others by promising to get sober from your addiction?*

4. *In what practical ways have you declared, "I can do this by myself!" instead of relying on God? Describe any attempts you've made to achieve sobriety by yourself. Describe, too, the results.*

5. *Outline what it will look like to totally surrender control to Christ.*

PRINCIPLE THREE

We make a list of our sins and weaknesses and confess those to a person of spiritual authority.

Telling the Truth: I Must Leave the Darkness

Assignment Two - Outlining Our Darkness

At this point in your program, you are waking up from the fog of your acting out behaviors. You're starting to get honest. Reality is sinking in, which might be frightening and discouraging. You probably were hoping for what AA calls "a softer gentler way." Be aware of your distorted thinking. Satan is likely telling you some lie like, "If this healing journey is so great, why do you feel so bad?"

Have you ever had an injury or some kind of surgery? You know that the recovery process is very often painful. You may feel a lot worse before you start feeling better. Healing from sexual trauma, sin, and addiction is no different.

Now, it's time to prepare an **honest inventory** of your life. When Jesus confronted a man who had been possessed by demons, he asked him, "What is your name?" The man said, "My name is Legion." It may seem that your sins are legion, and you may be overwhelmed by the enormity of your life's darkness.

Be aware that you're in a process of grieving - grieving all the painful experiences of the past. You're dealing with your shame and asking, "How could I have done such terrible things?" These feelings are normal. Though painful, they actually are signs of your transformation.

The best way to counter the darkness of your past is to continue to expose it to the light. You've been hiding your secret life for years, and your silence has been killing you. It's time to complete what the AA program calls a "searching and fearless moral inventory," and expose that outline of sins to the healing power of God's grace.

Instructions about Your Inventory

In preparing this inventory or outline, it's perhaps easiest to divide your life into stages and categories. As you examine the various areas of sin in your life, remember the words of Paul concerning his sinful nature. He wrote about *not* doing the things he *wanted* to do, and about *doing* the things he *didn't* want to do. Paul is describing sins of *commission* and sins of *omission*. Think not only about the sins you've done, but also about the good that you haven't done. Include your actions or lack of actions, but also outline your negative or sinful thoughts and your lack of positive ones.

Divide your life into stages much like the way you created the timeline for your first assignment in this *L.I.F.E. Recovery Guide.* **One simple division would be these areas: childhood, adolescence, teenage, young adult, mid-life, and senior years.** (Obviously, some of you haven't reached all of these stages).

Next, think about categories of your life such as these: ***family, education, social relationships, job or vocation, hobbies or recreation, sexuality, and your spiritual life.*** Some of your work will duplicate the sexual and relationship history you prepared earlier. That's fine. *This inventory, though, will be much broader than just your sexual behaviors. The intention is to outline every aspect of the sin in your life.* Explore every nook and cranny of your soul. Leave nothing hidden in the dark recesses of your spirit. The chart inserted below can be used to check the areas where you have completed your inventory work. The unmarked areas will be more visible to pick up where you left off.

Principle 3.2	Childhood	Teenage	Young Adult	Mid-Life	Senior
Family					
Education					
Social					
Job					
Recreation					
Sexuality					
Spirituality					

You may be overwhelmed by the variety or complexity of thoughts. Keep it simple. **Start journaling about one age and one category, and then move on to another.** Grow yourself up in your outline year by year, or at least stage by stage. Like all of the assignments in this workbook, this isn't a one-time exercise. It should be a living, changing document. You may update your inventory whenever a new memory or insight surfaces, even if that's years down the road.

Add examples (or even categories) as you think of them. You may have lied about many things or done a variety of crazy behaviors. In my story, for example, as a teenager I often acted out sexually when I was supposed to be babysitting. I'd make the kids go to bed early so my boyfriend could come over, then I'd lie to my dad about whether a guy had visited. In this single example, I was a sexual sinner, an irresponsible employee of my charges' parents, and a liar. Have you done anything similar? Did you ever cheat on a test or your income tax, take something that wasn't yours, or tell a lie to gain approval from others? *Whatever the sin, include it in your inventory.*

Sample Section of Inventory

> *You'll probably find it easier to write out your inventory in paragraph or list form, rather than trying to create a table of ages and categories. Use this sample from part of my own inventory as an idea to get you started, but don't hesitate to adapt this format or craft your own.*

MARNIE: YOUNG ADULT YEARS: Ages 20-25

This period of my life was tumultuous and chaotic. I married; my addiction escalated; I separated from my husband; went crazy with acting out; reconciled for a time; resumed having affairs; divorced; then quickly remarried.

AGE 20-21:

FAMILY: About three months before my marriage to Bob, I realized I was really getting married just to get away from home. I didn't have the courage to admit that insight and call off the wedding. Instead, I allowed my dad to placate me with reassurances that most brides had pre-wedding jitters. After the marriage failed, I lied to myself by blaming my father for pushing me to go through with it, rather than accepting responsibility for my fear and avoidance.

PERSONAL: I was more concerned about enjoying the spotlight as the bride of the decade than I was in being honest with myself or my future husband. I focused on making all the externals of the ceremony perfect, while I ignored the imperfections of my heart. Appearance is what mattered the most.

EDUCATION/JOB: I was finishing my senior year in college when I got married, and immediately after the honeymoon, I began student teaching. I felt desperate to do a good job – no, to be the *best* student teacher my professor had ever supervised. It was the same old drive to earn love and respect through my accomplishments. My job of student teaching took priority over everything, including my new husband. It became my total focus, at the expense of my relationships with everyone, including God. I was obsessed with my students and with teaching.

SEXUAL/RELATIONSHIP BEHAVIOR: I told God I wanted to do the right thing as a Christian wife, and Bob and I even chose to be abstinent in the months before the wedding as proof of my commitment. I promised God to be faithful to my husband, and for a while, I was. Within months, though, I was frustrated with Bob and dissatisfied with my life. Our sexual relationship was infrequent and boring. After the excitement of different partners, I felt cheated. Soon I began flirting with one of Bob's good friends. I fantasized about sleeping with him, and eventually I did – on the first anniversary of my wedding. I blamed Bob for our problems and chose to vent my anger by acting out on that significant day. I always thought that getting married would stop my promiscuity, but I was wrong. After that first slip, my addiction took off once again.

FINANCIAL: As newlyweds, money was tight. I was spoiled from spending my father's money at will, and I resented having to live on a budget. So I "stole" from our grocery money each week to go out with my girlfriends, while I hassled Bob for spending an extra dime.

Age 22

FAMILY: My family now consisted of just Bob, and ....etc., etc.

Continue your outline of your sins and shortcomings.

Take note of this important boundary: **This is not an exercise in which you describe in a grandiose way what a terrific sinner you are.**   This assignment isn't a competition to discover the most depraved person in the group. (The apostle Paul already claimed the title "chief of sinners"). Sometimes when an addict writes her inventory, it seems she's bragging about how terrible she was, so that her current state of sobriety will seem all the more amazing. False remorse is just another form of manipulation.

Also, when you're sharing about your assignment in your L.I.F.E. Recovery Group, please heed an additional word of caution. Observe appropriate boundaries the way you did when you shared your sexual and relationship history. **Don't be graphic in describing your sexual behaviors**, because you don't want to trigger (or educate) other members of the group.

This is a long assignment, and you'll probably fill pages and pages of work. Don't worry about leaving things out. The first time you compile your inventory, you may only hit the basics. You can go back and get more detailed later. Remember that you're practicing getting honest and you're taking many risks. Recovery is a process.

As you work on this assignment, be sure to take frequent breaks. Talk to a sister in recovery and get some support and encouragement. Be gentle with yourself. Remember again, *no sin can separate us from the love of God.* He does not throw stones. The sacrifice of Christ' blood cleanses us from all sin and makes us pure and holy in God's eyes. Allow His enduring love to comfort and sustain you as you humbly outline the failures of your life. God promises to transform you into the "newness of life."

Writing Exercise: Your Inventory

> *This exercise isn't a simple 1-2-3 list like some of the assignments. Read the instructions and suggestions in the following paragraphs, then begin outlining the sins in your life. It may help to use the sample journal section printed after the text which describes how to complete this exercise. Any way you organize your work is fine. The important thing is to write it down.*

PRINCIPLE FOUR

We seek accountability and to build our character as children of God.

Growing in Transformation: I Mature in Character

Assignment Two – Assessing Our Character

In addition to practicing accountability, women of integrity are women of character.

Character refers to the kind of people we are even when there *isn't* accountability. Character is the way we live when we know no one is watching or will find out. The apostle Paul, in Galatians, describes a character marked by integrity. He outlines the disposition of the sinful nature, and contrasts it with the makeup of a life lived in the Spirit:

> *The acts of the sinful nature are obvious: sexual immorality, impurity and debauchery; idolatry and witchcraft; hatred, discord, jealousy, fits of rage, selfish ambition, dissensions, factions and envy; drunkenness, orgies, and the like. I warn you, as I did before, that those who live like this will not inherit the kingdom of God. But the fruit of the Spirit is love, joy, peace, patience, kindness, goodness, faithfulness, gentleness and self-control. Against such things there is no law. Those who belong to Christ Jesus have crucified the sinful nature with its passions and desires. Since we live by the Spirit, let us keep in step with the Spirit. Let us not become conceited, provoking and envying each other.* (Galatians 5:19-26 NIV)

This verse is the theme of Principle Four. Working on the fruits of the Spirit will be a lifetime journey, which in spiritual terms is a process referred to as "sanctification." If, then, this process won't be completed in this lifetime, there's no way you will "complete" this assignment. But you can get started.

The Angry (Wounded) Heart

Since anger, along with loneliness, is the main emotion that drives sexual addiction, it's a good place to start. You'll notice how quickly Paul talks about anger in the passage above after he's described sexual immorality. Paul uses a number of words to break down "anger:" hatred, discord, jealousy, fits of rage, selfish ambition, dissensions, factions and envy.

These words are all obviously different, but their root is the same: a wounded heart that's angry about not being loved and nurtured. Realize that we all need to be affirmed, praised,

121

heard, touched in healthy ways, adored, and included in a healthy community. When we don't feel we're getting these things, we can become angry like a little child who's having a temper tantrum. In fact, if you're like me, there's a lot about your acting out that was very juvenile, exactly like a temper tantrum. Anger and a desperate need to get our needs met will lead to our being ambitious, envious, jealous and competitive. We'll have fits of rage, dissensions and lots of discord.

Anger can come out in a lot of ways. Sometimes it's direct; at other times it's indirect, like through sarcasm. We might get angry at someone who doesn't deserve it, because whatever he or she said or did reminded us of an older wound and an older anger, perhaps even unconsciously.

It is often important to identify who caused our original pain. Take a moment and ask God to teach you if your anger is older than the current situation - that is, if your anger at this person is really a reminder of an older wound. One way to identify older emotions is to ask yourself, "How old am I feeling right now?" You may be surprised to discover you feel like you're very young. You feel small and vulnerable and perhaps helpless. One symptom of responding in the moment to a much older situation is if painful memories come up for you. If you ask the right questions, memories of the original wound might surface. Don't be afraid of these memories. They're cleansing.

If you find that your anger is really out of control, you may need to work with a Christian therapist who can help discover its root. You may find that simply talking about your anger with trusted people will help dissipate it. Writing about the anger is another good way of expressing it. Remember, *anger can't be suppressed*; it will always come out sooner or later, usually in unhealthy ways.

Often therapy and support revolves around understanding how we were wounded and feeling the freedom to express anger at those who wounded us. These steps are an important part of the journey. They allow us to know that we didn't deserve the things that happened to us. They are ways we grieve, and therefore, heal.

Writing Exercises: Your Anger

For now, make a list of those whom you know you're angry with. Identify the people and write specifically what you're angry about. Share these memories with your group and ask them for feedback about any anger you might be showing today. Could it be related to these older situations?

Our Anger at God

When you're exploring your anger at others, don't forget about being angry with God. In the pain of my addiction, I was often angry with God. Many times I had prayed for Him to remove all lustful thoughts and temptations from my life. I wanted to be magically healed or delivered. Even as a child I was angry with God for "taking" my mother and leaving me alone. I was angry God didn't prevent me from all harm. Later, as I grew up and even since I became a Christian, I could get angry with God about anything that didn't go right in my life.

And I stayed totally stuck in my anger with God. Of course, I didn't know it was OK to be angry with God. I thought my feelings were just one more item in a long list of strikes against me. I stuffed my anger deep inside my heart and never shared it with anyone.

Perhaps you've felt the same way. You've believed it was wrong to be angry with God. If so, get out your Bible and read some of the Psalms that describe how angry King David felt with God at times. God doesn't ask us to squash our feelings, even the "bad" ones.

Writing Exercise:
Your Anger at God

Write a second list of reasons you've felt angry with God.

So now you have two lists of anger to share with your group. What do you do next?

I'm going to make a radical suggestion that might surprise you: **Decide to forgive every person on your list**. You might respond, "What? You just told me to be angry with these people, and now you're telling me to forgive them. I don't feel like doing that! Besides, none of them has asked for my forgiveness." This reaction is common, but it also springs from a misunderstanding about forgiveness.

Understanding Forgiveness

Forgiving someone else is for *your* emotional healing, not theirs. You can *decide* at some point to forgive even if you don't *feel* like it. Often, we get this order backward. We think we have to feel like doing something before we do it. Actually, the reverse sequence is true: Our feelings may *follow* our decisions; not the other way around. An AA slogan is, "Take the right action, and the feelings will follow." *Forgiveness is an act of the will*. Healing emotions may follow immediately or only after considerable time has passed.

Some of us have been counseled not to give up our anger too quickly because if we do, we'll stay vulnerable to being hurt again. Don't confuse forgiveness with your ongoing need to set healthy boundaries. You can be safe and still forgive. In fact, *forgiveness doesn't necessarily mean the reconciliation of relationship*. Your boundaries may include not having contact with those who hurt you, and that's OK.

Another mistake we make is in thinking that forgiveness is a one-time event. You may have to forgive someone over and over again, which was certainly true for me. As I saw my daughter grow up and mature, I understood what my life might have been like if I hadn't been sexually abused, and I had to choose to forgive my perpetrator repeatedly as my daughter went through various stages unburdened by the baggage of abuse.

Writing Exercise

> *Write in your journal about a specific decision you've made to forgive someone. Describe the offense or wound, then write a statement of forgiveness to the one who hurt you. You might begin, "I choose to forgive _____ for _____."*

Here's the bottom line: Forgiving someone is a *spiritual act of obedience*. It's what Jesus tells us to do: *"Forgive us our debts (trespasses) as we forgive our debtors."* Do you want to be forgiven for your sexual sins? Practice forgiving others for whatever hurt they have caused you. When you've made a decision to forgive, then you must *act* like you have. Remember that you can still have your boundaries and you may still experience strong feelings, but you *act* in a way that brings honor to God. Refer back to the fruits of the Spirit that Paul talks about: patience, kindness, goodness, gentleness, and self-control.

We can choose to act according to these fruits as an act of obedience to God, no matter how we feel.

With God, you, of course, don't need to forgive Him. But you do need to work on accepting that everything God has allowed to happen to you has been for a reason. Just because you don't understand the reason yet, doesn't mean there isn't one. Today, I think back on all the things I was angry with God about, and I see that from some of them, I learned some great lessons. Would I take that knowledge away? Not on your life! I've discovered that the times I'm most angry or disappointed with God have ultimately been the ones that are the most character-building. Growth is usually painful.

Writing Exercise

> *Reflect in your journal about some of the lessons you've learned through adversity. How have these experiences built your character?*

Anger Fueled by Fear or Anxiety

Often, we are angry because we are *afraid*. We don't feel safe and we worry about the future. Our wounds from the past may have impaired our ability to feel safe. We've been hurt and abandoned, and we have memories of fear and anxiety. Something in the present can easily trigger us back to those older feelings. Fear and anxiety feed upon themselves and can create a vicious cycle of obsessive thinking about danger.

It's important to understand the difference between anxiety and fear. *Anxiety* is usually about something more global or general in nature – like being totally alone, having no meaning in your life, experiencing death, and being judged or condemned. *Fear* is usually about something specific.

For example, I'm generally afraid of not having my house clean and in order. I can become quite obsessed and worried about these things when they don't get done. (Ask my husband or children.) I can get angry at myself for not doing them or at others (like my family) for not helping me. The fact is that taking care of my house symbolizes my worth as a person. It sounds silly, doesn't it? But how many of the things you worry about have been labeled "silly" by others?

Today I understand that my obsession with the state of my house goes back to my family's number one rule: "Appearances are all-important. If you can't be perfect, you must at least look perfect." Our "silly" obsessions are perhaps symbols of deep anxieties that we carry from our wounds. When you begin to understand that even little things can trigger you into deeper anxieties, you can realize why there're times when even little things bother you so much. An important part of assessing our character is understanding these "buttons" that trigger us into anger, anxiety, or fear.

If you're really impaired by anxiety, the antidote may taking medication for a time. Don't be afraid of this approach; many people may need this help. Some of us have genetic predispositions in our neurochemistry to have more difficulty with fear and anxiety. Others have experienced such profound trauma that they need extra help to feel safe. Neither situation is something to be ashamed of. It's simply a part of who we are. Part of maturing in character may be challenging our pride or embarrassment at requiring this level of help.

Writing Exercise: **Your Fear**	*Write in your journal about the last time you felt really afraid. Can you identify any words or events that triggered the feeling?*

Fellowship: An Antidote to Fear

Another important antidote to fear and anxiety is the safety you're beginning to experience in your L.I.F.E. Group. We learn to be afraid in unhealthy relationships, and we can learn to feel safe in healthy ones. Assessing our character may involve recognizing how our trust of others is impaired because of our woundedness. Finding fellowship through a support group can be a huge step of faith.

During check-in time at every group be sure to report on any fears or anxieties you're having. Begin to think about what might help you to feel safe. At the appropriate times get some feedback from your accountability group about safety.

The main antidote to fear and anxiety is *developing a greater dependence on God.* The journey of transformation and recovery is a spiritual journey. As many times as necessary, refer back to the work that you need to do in Principle Two, and remind yourself of the ongoing discipline you'll need to grow in your relationship with Christ.

Principle Five

We explore the damage we have done, accept responsibility, and make amends for our wrongs.

Demonstrating Real Change: I Accept Responsibility

Principle Five marks a turning point in your journey of transformation. Here's a review of your work to this point as guided by the first four Principles: You admit the unmanageability of your life because of sexual sin and your inability to solve the problem on your own. Next, you choose to surrender totally to Christ and to seek God's will for your life on a daily basis. You inventory your history with complete honesty and reveal the truth through specific confession to another person. Then you address your flaws and inadequacies of character by entering into relationships of accountability.

These first four Principles are vital in forming the foundation for genuine, lasting change. You examine the depth of your sinful nature and your need for God. You take the huge steps of telling the truth and asking for help.

The journey this far, though, is also largely self-focused. These examinations and confessions and submission to accountability require great introspection. You're looking inward and exploring your own life, behavior, mind and heart.

Principle Five expands your investigation. It challenges you to look outside of yourself and consider the ways your sexual sin has impacted others. You admit that you're not isolated in your sin and that it has repercussions for others. People in your life are affected by your addiction. Your actions have caused pain for many, probably more than you'd like to think. In a variety of ways, your behavior and character flaws have harmed others. The process of Principle Five begins with a thorough assessment of the damage caused by your sexual sin, its consequences and your character flaws. Like Nehemiah, you venture outside yourself to survey the damage that exists in your environment. You observe the fallout of your life. You catalog the pain you've caused for others. You look unflinchingly at the harm you've brought about.

Assignment Two - Planning Amends

Assessing the damage as a result of your sexual sin and listing those whom you've harmed is only the starting point. In fact, those acknowledgments are hollow if you stop there. The list you've created serves as the springboard into action – specific, identifiable action. Assignment Two of Principle Five prepares you for taking the actions of *restitution*.

First, I need to define what I mean by making restitution. The Twelve Step programs refer to these actions as making amends for our wrongs. *In simple terms, making amends means offering an apology for the harm you've caused.* It's saying, "I'm sorry," with humility and without any expectation of receiving forgiveness. But making amends is also backing up the apology with specific attempts to make things right. Willingness to provide restitution is a good indicator of the genuineness of your apology.

Making Direct Amends

Addicts can offer two kinds of amends. The first is **direct amends**, where you provide restitution specifically to the person you've damaged. One by one, you approach the individuals who have suffered because of your sexual sin, and you express your remorse for what you've done and for the pain it caused. If there is some overt way to right the wrong, you suggest it, and then provide it if you are allowed.

Zacchaeus, the tax collector mentioned in Luke 19, provides a great example of making amends through specific restitution. He had apparently used the authority of his position to collect more money than citizens owed. After his encounter with Jesus, Zacchaeus promised to pay people back four times the amount he had cheated from them. (See Luke 19: 1-9 for the Biblical account of Zacchaeus' story).

Making Indirect Amends

A second type of amends is vicarious restitution (often called **indirect amends**). This approach is used when it's impossible or inappropriate to make direct amends. Perhaps you don't know how to contact someone you've harmed, or maybe the person has died. In some cases you may not even know the identity of those you've hurt, especially if your acting out has been extensive. These are situations where you can make vicarious amends. For example, you could donate funds to help the victims of sexual sin receive counseling or treatment. One male addict I know routinely pays the way (anonymously) for one person to attend a Healing for Spouses program offered through Bethesda Workshops. This addict sees his donation as an on-going way to help others who have suffered because of their mate's sexual addiction, just as his wife did. The possibilities of vicarious repayment are endless.

A second situation that warrants indirect restitution is if it would be harmful to make direct amends. You take this path when it would be more injurious to interact specifically with someone you've harmed. Certain affair situations provide clear examples of cases where it's inappropriate to make direct amends. One would be if the wife of a man you've had an affair with doesn't know about your involvement. It would be harmful for her to learn about the betrayal through your confession and apology. She needs to learn of the affair from her own husband, not through you. Likewise, it would be wrong to apologize to the children of an affair partner, unless you were certain they were already aware of the infidelity and were old enough to understand your comments.

In these kinds of circumstances, devise some way of making indirect amends to injured parties. Get creative. After all of the thought and energy you've spent figuring out how to hide your sexual sin, put your creativity to positive use and come up with some constructive ways to counteract some of the damage you've done.

Explore Your Motives

Let me caution you about your work on this Principle. It's important you carefully examine why you want to make amends in each case. As addicts, we're used to manipulating outcomes, and it's possible you hope to benefit in some way by saying you're sorry. Maybe you think you'll be let off the hook or get back in someone's good graces. Those are flawed motives that will taint your actions. Refer again to the story of the Prodigal Son in Luke 15. He wasn't trying to regain his status as a son. In fact, he was willing to be a lowly servant to his father. Be unflinching as you examine your heart for any possible selfish motives in making amends. Be courageous.

Scrutinize your motives for the reason behind your desire to make amends to each person on your list. Here are some possible motivations:

- to prevent or stop someone from being angry at you

- to make yourself feel better for what you've done

- to influence someone to trust you again

- to manipulate someone's pity or compassion

- to transfer blame by saying, "I'm sorry, but I wouldn't have done this if you hadn't done …."

- to attempt to avoid consequences by expressing regret

- to accept full responsibility for the harm you've caused

- to demonstrate empathy for those you've hurt

- to rectify your damage to the extent possible

Writing Exercise: Your Motives

Journal about your true motives for making amends in each case. Pray for discernment and purity of heart.

On the other hand, be optimistic and thankful for the changes God is prompting in you. As you've worked through these principles of being faithful and true, you've progressed from a place of denial to the point of being willing to accept full responsibility for what you've done and the harm you've caused. This difficult work in Principle Five is one more step in your transformation journey. Remember, God will be faithful to finish the good work He has started in your heart (Philippians 1:6).

Plan specifically how you'll go about making amends, both directly and vicariously. For each person, first determine if direct amends or indirect amends is most appropriate. Write the best method beside each name.

Writing Exercises: Your Plan

Name of Person Harmed	*Kind of Amends (Direct or Indirect)*
_____	_____
_____	_____
_____	_____
_____	_____
_____	_____

Then develop a plan. Who will you approach first? How will you contact that person? What will you say? What action will you take?

Identify the first three people to whom you can make direct amends:	*Then identify three ways of making indirect amends:*
1. _____	1. _____
2. _____	2. _____
3. _____	3. _____
Write your specific plan in your journal. Be as detailed as you can.	Write out that plan, too.

Talk with your sponsor and L.I.F.E. Recovery Group about your list of those you've harmed, the damage you've done, and your plan for making amends. Ask for feedback. Are there any obvious omissions to your list? Are your motives as pure as you can make them? Is your plan appropriate and reasonable for the person and situation?

> *Make an appointment to meet with your sponsor or determine when you'll share with your L.I.F.E. Recovery Group. Record that time in your journal.*

DO NOT TAKE ANY ACTION
without first sharing your plan with your accountability system.

Principle Six

In fellowship with others we develop honest, intimate relationships, where we celebrate our progress and continue to address our weaknesses.

Living in Fellowship: I Cannot Succeed Alone

Congratulations on getting this far in your journey to maintain integrity in your sexual behavior and relationships. I know it's taken courage, perseverance and commitment. In many ways it may have been harder than you anticipated. You've experienced many feelings that may be new to you. You've had to humble yourself in admitting the full truth about your history, your thoughts and your offenses. But with God's help, you've done it. You've told your story of sexual sin. You've decided you want to get well and have surrendered your life to Christ. You've accepted accountability from a sponsor and perhaps have begun working with a counselor. You're willing to make amends to those you have harmed. I pray you're beginning to have a deeper sense of God's power and presence in your life.

Principle Six guides you into a way of living that involves genuine connection with others, instead of the isolation you've probably known. The foundation for this work comes from one of Mark Laaser's core teaching principles:

Fellowship is equal to freedom from lust.

It's probably hard for you to believe this promise. You may have been alone for years as you've hidden your sexual secrets from others. You've never known the joy of a supportive community. Your shame kept you from connecting with others, while it continued to fuel your lust and sexual sin. (You also probably can't imagine a life free from fantasy and lust, which have felt like your constant companions for as long as you can remember.) Principle Six offers a path out of your isolation, which in turn, is the road to sexual integrity.

Hopefully, you're already enjoying some of the benefits of fellowship through your L.I.F.E. group. You're bonding with other Christian women who've faced similar struggles and seek to live in sexual freedom and purity. You're beginning to experience both the grace of God and the grace of other Christians who will love you despite your mistakes.

Assignment Two - Changing Our Cycle

By now the cycle of addiction as described by Patrick Carnes is a familiar diagram. This graphic outlines the woundedness, which is at the core of our disease, the shame, our preoccupation and fantasy, our rituals, then our acting out, and of course, our despair. (Though I doubt I need to remind you about this cycle, you can refer to Assignment Two of Principle One for more details.)

I pray you're maintaining uninterrupted sobriety. I hope you're also experiencing some core changes of life and character. The journey you're making is about so much more than sexual integrity. **It's about the transformation of someone who is surrendered to Christ.**

Review the commission of Romans 12:

> *"Therefore, I urge you, [sisters], in view of God's mercy, to offer your bodies as living sacrifices, holy and pleasing to God – this is your spiritual act of worship. Do not conform any longer to the pattern of this world, but be transformed by the renewing of your mind."* (Romans 12: 1-2)

God is after so much more than our sexual purity. He longs to transform our sinful natures into a closer likeness of His Son. **He desires our heart.**

One of my favorite verses is Psalm 37:4:

> *"Delight in the LORD, and he will give you the desires of your heart."*

I'm ashamed to admit it, but in the darkness of my addiction, I clung to that verse as a promise that one day I'd receive the desire of my (sinful) heart, which was to be with my affair partner. But as God transformed my heart into delighting in *Him*, rather than in my own selfish wants, I discovered that He had, indeed, given me the desire of my heart. That promise came true because <u>God transformed my desire</u>, until what I wanted above all else was to be holy and whole before God.

To illustrate this transformation process, Mark Laaser created a cycle of recovery, which is diagrammed on the following page.

LAASER CYCLE OF RECOVERY

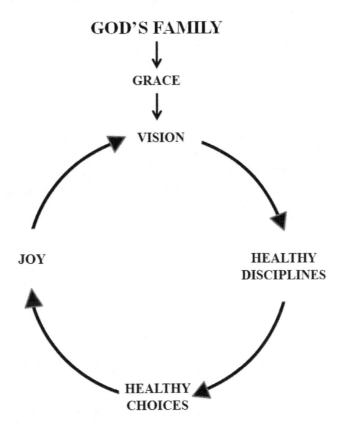

Instead of the addictive cycle of pain and sin, the transformed life of a new creature in Christ is characterized by this cycle of recovery. (We'll talk about vision in Assignment Three of Principle Seven.) Assignment Two, here, focuses on the main body of the cycle itself. It's actually just the visual representation of the behaviors I outlined in Assignment One. The checkpoints that make up the Daily Inventory are the Healthy Disciplines and Healthy Choices depicted in the cycle of recovery.

Review again the five core areas of healthy living that make up the Daily Inventory: physical, behavioral, personal, relational and spiritual. The items listed are examples of healthy disciplines, such as attending a L.I.F.E. Recovery Group meeting, calling your sponsor, or praying. These disciplines lead to healthy choices in behavior, thought, and character. Just like there's a predictable progression into sin, there's a known path of transformation. When you allow God to be in control of your life and heart, He can guide you into the pathway of joy as you grow in Him.

Being connected with the family of God provides the fellowship of healthy community. That's why I insist no one can ever recover alone. *God made us for relationship, which we obviously can't experience in isolation. We need each other.* It's partially through intimacy with others that we come to grow in intimacy with God.

When you live out the Principles of living in sexual purity, you invite sisters to be part of your journey of transformation, and you become part of theirs. You dare to admit your sins, ask for help, be accountable, accept responsibility, heal core wounds, and share the grace you've found in Christ. In healthy fellowship you find sisters and brothers in the family of God. You tell your secrets, expose your dark heart to the light and live in freedom everyday.

Writing Exercises: Changing Our Cycle

> **Write the names of three to four women who are part of your circle of fellowship. Write a sentence or two of gratitude for each one. Contact each sister this week and share what you've written about your thankfulness for her part in your life.**

List the healthy disciplines you commit to focus on this week. Identify one from each core area you need to improve.

1. Phy!
2. Beh:
3. Rela
4. Pers
5. Spir

> *Reflect on the positive changes in your life over the last several weeks. Record three or four instances of joy that are evidence of your healthy choices.*

PRINCIPLE SEVEN

As we live in sexual integrity, we carry the message of Christ's healing to those who still struggle, and we pursue a vision of God's purpose for our lives.

Finding a Purpose: I Have a Vision

Assignment Two - Sharing Your Pain

In Assignment One of Principle Seven, you made preparations to tell your story. Before you unleash yourself on others, take one more step. The goal of this assignment is to help you understand what God has been trying to teach you about Himself through your story.

I'm not saying that God sat up in heaven one day and decided to make you an addict or even simply to permit all these crazy things to happen to you. God allows us to have free will and to come to knowledge of Him through our own decisions. Amazingly, God designed life in such a way that our experiences can teach us powerful lessons about what He is really like. Our job is to listen.

Many books can be resources to help with this assignment. I would encourage you to read Henry Nouwen's book, *The Return of the Prodigal Son*. (The biblical account is found in Luke 15:11-32, but you probably already know the story.) In powerful and insightful ways, Nouwen's book describes the roles of the Prodigal Son, the father and the older brother.

How is it, do you think, that the father in this story was so understanding of the son? How is this earthly father able to be so forgiving? Isn't he like most other earthly fathers, who would react more harshly to a disgraceful son? One interpretation is that perhaps this father had his own sinful past. Perhaps he knew what it was like to make mistakes and to feel like he was in the "pig pen." Did this father's understanding of how all of us turn away from home allow him to take his son back in such a loving and gracious way? Clearly, in this parable Jesus illustrates the forgiving nature of God.

What's equally obvious is your own status as a Prodigal Son (or more accurately, a Prodigal Daughter). You acknowledged your sinful rebellion back in Principle One, and you've continued your journey of returning home – your path into L.I.F.E.

While the father was glad to welcome the prodigal home, not everyone had the same reaction. Do you remember the jealousy of the older brother when the wayward son returned? He was judgmental and angry. Does that reaction describe your attitude toward others still mired in the pig pen of sin? Do you at times feel superior because of your progress in turning your life around? Wouldn't you want to be like the gracious father and not the older brother? It's your own life experience that can teach you to be forgiving and encouraging to others.

I recommend another of Nouwen's books called *The Inner Voice of Love*. Nouwen personally experienced a time of great despair in his latter life. The word is that he, himself, struggled with some sexually sinful behavior. Eventually, he went on a personal retreat where he kept a journal, just as you've been doing. Nouwen's journal was later published as *The Inner Voice of Love*.

One of his reflections in that book is very powerful. Nouwen says we should allow our pain to become "*the* pain." He believes that all of us have experienced circumstances in our lives that create painful memories and feelings. It is our pain. Nouwen goes on to say, however, that if we only spend time dwelling on the unique circumstances that caused our pain, we'll fall short of really understanding it. We might believe, he says, that if our circumstances had been different, we might not have any pain. Better, he thinks, is to come to an understanding that our personal pain is our "opportunity" to experience the pain of all humanity.

Think about it. What has connected you with others in your life? Was it success? Have your various achievements really brought you the peace and serenity you've longed for? Have you felt connected by being on the winning team? Or have you felt more connected by getting honest in the last weeks with others who know what you've gone through? It seems to me that when we allow ourselves to share our suffering, we find true connection with other sufferers.

Another book with a similar message is Larry Crabb's *Shattered Dreams*. He describes our reactions when we become shattered by life experiences and how we come to true connection through our brokenness.

Consider these words of Jesus:

> *"Come to me, all you who are weary and burdened, and I will give you rest. Take my yoke upon you and learn from me, for I am gentle and humble in heart, and you will find rest for your souls. For my yoke is easy and my burden is light."* (Matthew 11:28-30 NIV)

As a woman who's struggled with your sexual and relationship behavior, you've lived that first part about being tired and stressed out. You've sought the rest that Jesus promises. But if you're like me, you've had difficulty understanding the last part about taking on Christ's yoke. Was His burden really light? It certainly doesn't seem "light" to me.

As God's son, Jesus gave up His status and became a man. As a human, Christ experienced the difficult things that we do. He was even afraid of the pain of his death and asked God, "If it be Your will, take this cup from me." Jesus felt abandoned in the Garden by His disciples. He was rejected and despised by His own people. He was tortured and put to a painful death. On the cross, He doubted and wondered where God had gone, until Jesus cried in despair, "Why have You forsaken me?" Christ knew the meaninglessness of hell, because He descended into its depths for three days.

When we're in relationship with Christ, we have a brother who knows how we feel. Do you remember what it was like to go to your first meeting, tell your story, and experience the huge relief that others understood? In that moment, did your burden feel lighter? That is what Jesus is asking us to do — take His burden, and allow your pain to be the pain of all humanity. It is also His pain, and He knows full well how it feels. After you've considered how your pain connects you with the pain of others, would you take away your past if you could? Do you see that perhaps it's allowed you to experience the pain of others who suffer? Your own pain has given you compassion and empathy for your spouse, your children, your brothers and sisters. Can you begin to believe that the pain of your "burden" has been a gift? How else would you begin to understand the gift of God's grace through His Son Jesus Christ?

Perhaps, it's time to stop feeling sorry for yourself. Do you see why some introduce themselves by saying, "Hi, my name is _____, and I'm a *grateful* recovering sex addict"? That statement is a testimony to the transforming power of God!

Writing Exercise

> ***Reflect and write in your journal about what your losses and pain have taught you about depending on God.***

Now, as you consider sharing your story, I ask you to reflect on any testimonies you've heard. Which ones have really been helpful and inspirational? Has it been those in which people bragged about how well they're doing, or has it been those in which people honestly and transparently told about their struggles and their pain? Perhaps it was a sister who was willing to tell you her story that got you to come to a L.I.F.E. Recovery Group meeting in the first place.

Would you like to give the gift of your story to someone else? Remember back to all those times when you longed to know that someone else understood what you were going through. By God's grace, someone came along, shared her story of brokenness and her healing, and now you're on the road to recovery, too. Right now, I'd bet that you know someone who needs to hear *your* story.

Consider people to whom you'd like to tell your story. They don't have to be possible or probable sex addicts. They just need to be people whom you know struggle. You may feel frightened at the idea of telling your story to "normal" (non-addicted) people. You may even be having a "shame attack" - that is, you're thinking, "It'll be hard enough to tell my story to other sex addicts. How could I tell it to *anyone*?" Relax for now. You'll probably begin sharing your story only with those you know are relatively safe. As you grow in your recovery and transformation, you'll find others.

In my own journey, there have been many times I've told my story to a woman who was a sexual abuse survivor, a depressed woman contemplating suicide, or someone going through a divorce, only to discover she could relate to my experiences of sex addiction, too. My belief is that the Holy Spirit will direct your story telling. God will bring people to you, and you'll feel that tug at your heart alerting you they need to hear your story. Trust the prompting of those feelings and be of good courage.

Now, I don't mean you should rush out and tell your story to everyone. (That's not practicing healthy boundaries.) You may have that temptation, because part of you just wants to tell the whole world and get the truth out there. You might think spilling all would be a great catharsis - a cleansing of your soul. But you need to be careful so that you don't share indiscriminately with those who might not be safe. When in doubt, always check out your desire to share your story with your group or your accountability network. Get their feedback about the appropriateness of sharing with a specific person. On the other hand, your group might also be able to encourage you when you need support.

Writing Exercise: Sharing Your Story

> *List the names of four people who might need to hear your story:*
>
>   *1.*
>
>   *2.*
>
>   *3.*
>
>   *4.*
>
> *Keep track in your journal of those times when you do share about your journey. Record your feelings about what it was like to offer your "experience, strength, and hope." Describe the other person's reaction.*

Do you see, again, that working this assignment of Principle Seven is a lifetime journey?

PRINCIPLE ONE

We admit that we have absolutely no control of our lives. Sexual sin has become unmanageable.

Confronting Reality: I'm Shackled in My Own Prison

Congratulations! Despite long years of deceit, lies, denial, minimization, fears, shame, and manipulation, you have picked up this *L.I.F.E. Recovery Guide* or have come to a L.I.F.E. Recovery Group meeting. You have been wanting to, thinking that perhaps you should, pondering if it was the right thing. You have resisted, found excuses, wondered who would find out, and worried about the consequences of getting honest. You've thought that no one would really understand. You've either believed that you have done the worst things possible (things no one else has ever done) or you've thought your stuff is not so bad - that you really don't need to come to a meeting and admit you need help. Hear these words:

Welcome.

You're in the right place.

We're glad you're here.

Imagine what it must have been like for the Prodigal Son. He just wanted to be home. He didn't think he deserved to return to his earlier status as a son because his sins were so great. He hoped merely to be like one of his father's hired servants. Maybe you're like that: You're just glad to be alive and able to get to a meeting. You'd like to simply be quiet and belong. The Prodigal Son's father, however, rushed out to meet him and prepared a great feast. That is what it is like with God. We want to be "imitators of God, just like little children."

You probably feel like a Prodigal Daughter. And in the view of society (as well as the church), that's much worse than being a Prodigal Son. Only men are supposed to struggle with sexual sin. You can't believe other Christian women hide similar secrets. You're convinced you must be all alone. Like a fearful child, you expect to be ridiculed or shunned if you show up at a L.I.F.E. Recovery Group meeting. You imagine the meeting notice is actually a mistake and that no other women will be waiting.

Well, dear sister, your fears are unfounded. It may feel like you're a little girl who has just come on the bus or into the lunchroom or onto the playground and you're expecting to be rejected or at least ignored. Instead, we rush over to greet you! We've been where you've been. We understand your pain and your fears. We're glad you've come. We can't prepare a great feast, but we can go to coffee later.

Your first assignment is just to get honest. We know that the greatest enemy of sexual purity is silence. We also know how carefully you've guarded your sexual secrets. It's hard to imagine letting them out. There are demons in your mind telling you, "No! You can't talk about that. Someone will go running and screaming out of the room!" We encourage you to confront those demons. Those voices have kept you shackled in your pain for too long. We know, because we're on a similar journey of learning to live in freedom every day. We want you to tell us how bad it got and what it was like to feel powerless over your life. Chances are that others in your group have done some of the same things.

Though you feel like a Prodigal Daughter, there is nothing - certainly no sexual sin - that separates you from the love of God. No matter what you've thought or what you've done, it's time to come home to the heavenly Father who loves you and is longing for your freedom.

The assignment that you are about to undertake will take great courage. It will be a risk and a challenge. Don't turn back now. Keep putting one foot in front of the other and head for home. The freedom you'll experience is worth all it will take to get there.

Assignment Three - Identifying our Roots and Desires

As you've worked through the Principles you should now have a pretty good grasp on how truly powerless you have been over your sexual addiction. I hope you're making progress in accepting responsibility for your sinful behavior, seeking accountability, and connecting in genuine fellowship with others. It's time now for you to examine the core causes that have contributed to your addiction.

We suggest that you have a solid foundation of sobriety and support before you begin probing into the underlying issues. You may have already noticed in your work thus far that many feelings have come up for you that you've historically sought to medicate.

Stop for a moment. Stirring up painful feelings may seem like a problem to you. Perhaps you've been one of those Christians who has believed that once you start making the right decisions, like getting sober, everything will just automatically get better. You may have thought that you won't experience negative consequences, that your spouse would immediately start trusting you, that you wouldn't lose important relationships or face financial chaos. Most of all, you've thought that you would be "happy." You're disappointed and discouraged that you continue to feel tough emotions.

Welcome to reality! Your journey toward living in freedom every day is just that – a journey. The road won't always be clear or the way smooth. Making right choices won't exempt you from painful consequences or difficult emotions. In fact, this beginning period of recovery is probably one of the hardest you'll ever experience. For so long your emotions have been covered by your acting out, until you probably didn't feel anything at all most of the time. And guess what? When you do begin to feel, the first emotions are almost always the painful ones.

The period of time between the third and the ninth months of recovery is a really dangerous time for a variety of reasons. First, you might be experiencing the violation of expectations that I just described, and your reaction might be anger. Perhaps you're saying to yourself, "What's the use of being in a healing journey if this is all I get? I thought my life would be better by now." You could also be angry about all the restrictions in your life because of your recovery program. There seem to be so many things that have been taken away. You may hate being an "addict." You believe you're not normal and you feel strange. You may be getting tired of all the hard work.

Relax. You are normal. Remember that even though you call yourself an addict now, that word doesn't define who you are. You are a precious child of God. You are fearfully and wonderfully made. Yes, you are a person who has suffered with an addiction, but you are much more than that. Be gentle with yourself.

Writing Exercise

In the first part of this assignment make a list of the good qualities about yourself. If you can't think of any, ask some of your group members to help you.

Now that you have reminded yourself of some of your positive attributes, you can move on. (However, don't forget that you need to work your program just as hard now as you did in the first few weeks.) It's time to go deeper into your thoughts and feelings. It's time to get to some of the root causes of your loneliness and anger.

Wounds From Your Family

Please start by doing some reading in other places about family of origin issues. There are a wide variety of good options. Check out the resource section on the L.I.F.E. Recovery website (www.freedomeveryday.org). If your group wants to be on the same page, read through Part Two (chapters 7–11) of my book *No Stones: Women Redeemed From Sexual Shame*. These chapters give an explanation of how families work and some of the mistakes they can make.

I think it's important to remind you of the purpose of this kind of work. It's not to blame our parents or others for our problems. Blaming doesn't solve anything. **The point is to gain understanding, which we can use to help us change our behavior and further our healing.**

Another significant reminder concerns the terms we use to describe our families. We sometimes refer to coming from an "unhealthy" or "dysfunctional" family and a "healthy" or "functional" family. Many of us have a hard time with those descriptions and feel put in a difficult position by those distinctions. We thought that we came from a rather nice family. Historically, we may have been protective of them and not very interested in getting into all these memories of problems.

This attitude is a natural resistance. We've been taught as Christians to love and honor our families. We do, in fact, love them and probably need them.

I believe that our thinking in these matters gets too black and white. Do we really need our families to be either "good" or "bad?" All families are families that do many good and loving things. All families also make mistakes. I know that I've made many mistakes as a mother. Does that make me a dysfunctional mom? I hope it makes me a mother who loves her kids and tries her best. I believe that in most cases, that description is true even of those parents who make horrendous mistakes. Some mothers and fathers are immature and selfish to the point where some really terrible things happen to the children in that home. But as you'll see as we outline the healing journey, we shouldn't get stuck in trying to decide how good or bad our parents are. That judgment is ultimately up to God.

In my experience, some of us feel "family of origin shame," which can take two different paths. One is to think that we come from the worst possible family. Our story is really bad, our parents really terrible, and our wounds really damaging. We might even be tempted to think that it's no wonder we did so many sexual sins, because our history is such a nightmare. We can also get competitive in thinking that our story is the "worst."

The other path is to feel shame because we can't think of that many problems in our family. Now we're in trouble of a different sort. How could we have done such terrible sexual sins when there doesn't seem to be any root cause? We start worrying that the problem is totally within ourselves, and that thought is horribly shameful. We might even think about "inventing" some stories about our family so that we can "fit in."

Even the therapeutic community is concerned about this last possibility. There's a debate that goes on about something called "False Memory Syndrome." The belief by some is that therapists can prompt a person to create memories that didn't really happen. An untrained or unwise counselor may say something like, "You have all the symptoms of being sexually abused. Are you sure your father didn't do something to you?" If a therapist has ever said to you, "Since 80% of all sex addicts are sexual abuse survivors, you must be one, too," you need to be extremely careful.

Over the years I've found that the best approach is always the way of prayer. Take a moment every time you begin work on this assignment and ask God to help you remember the events of the past that have harmed you. Tell God you are willing to heal from these experiences and that you aren't just looking for excuses. Admit to God that you have a lot of pain, loneliness, and anger and ask Him to show you its origin. Always be in counseling or in groups that remind you to do this kind of prayer. Therapists, pastors, and groups can only guide and encourage you in this prayerful journey; they can't suggest to you what really happened.

As you work through this material about your family, let me summarize some of the issues that you should be aware of:

- The **rules** that existed in your family. Think of examples of how your family taught you to express your feelings, to talk, and to accept responsibility. Or did your family *not* talk, not feel, blame, minimize, or deny responsibility?

- The **roles** that were played out in your family. Examples include the heroine or saint, the little princess, the scapegoat, the mascot, the doer, the martyr, and the peacemaker.

- Did your family observe healthy **boundaries**? Did you feel safe? Did you feel loved, protected, nurtured, and affirmed?

- Were there **addictions** present in your family? Some of these might have been substances and others might have been behaviors. If there was an addict, who was the enabler?

- Were you emotionally, physically, sexually, or spiritually **abused** in an invasive way?

- Are there ways you were **abandoned**? Do you feel that you got what you needed? Were you affirmed, heard, protected, touched, and desired? Understand that it's often hard to identify ways we may have been abandoned in a family (even if both parents are present in the home), because how do you know you missed something that you never had?

Writing Exercises: Your Family

- *List the main <u>rules</u> that existed in your family.*

- *What were the primary <u>roles</u> you played in your family? What roles did others play?*

- *Describe the <u>boundaries</u> in your family. Were they too loose? Too rigid? Or a combination of both?*

- *List the <u>addictions</u> present in your family and the identity of the addict(s).*

- *What forms of <u>abuse</u> did you experience? Who was the perpetrator(s)?*

- *In what ways were you <u>abandoned</u>? When did you feel lonely, frightened, left out,*

NOTE: *Remember, you may need more information about family dynamics in order to understand them fully and to complete this writing assignment. Refer to* No Stones, *Part Two, or a similar source for a thorough explanation.*

Connecting with the Comforter

I know I'm asking you to do some very painful work. You may resist delving into these feelings. You may even be feeling anxious or unsafe. I encourage you to pause for a few moments and do an imagery exercise at this point. It's important to only undertake this work with the comfort and presence of your heavenly Father.

Create, if you can, an image in your mind. Do you remember the Bible story recorded in Matthew 19: 13-15 about the little children Jesus welcomed after the disciples had tried to keep them away? Imagine that you are one of those children. You really want to sit on Jesus' lap, but there is something that keeps you from doing so. Perhaps you're afraid you'll bother him, or worse, that you'll be ridiculed or rejected. You can't imagine that Jesus really wants to spend time with you.

Then, in your mind, let your eyes meet those of Jesus and hear His words of invitation, *"Come to me."* The Lord reaches out His hand and beckons you closer. When you climb up on His lap, imagine that He comforts you and tells you how much He loves you.

Then Jesus gently asks, *"What are you feeling, my child? What is it like to be you?"* Remember, you aren't an adult, but a child. Be honest with Jesus. Tell Him about your experiences growing up in your family. Share your hurts and fears. He can hear you and understand. He already knows what it was like for you. He wants you to say it.

Writing Exercise

Describe in your journal what this conversation with Jesus was like. Write the things you told Him. Take as long as you need and simply allow the feelings to surface. When you're through, consider making a special effort to talk with someone from your L.I.F.E. Recovery Group about this exercise.

Trauma Reactions

The principle of why we do this hard work is simple. The aftereffects of trauma don't go away on their own. Painful memories have a way of surfacing and creating feelings. Have you ever had someone like your spouse say, "You're overreacting!" or "Why did something so trivial create such a large reaction?" When the intensity of our response doesn't match the precipitating event, it's a clear sign we've been triggered into the pain of the past.

Sometimes, these reactions to the past come in forms other than over-reaction. You may think that someone is angry with you, and they say they're not. In that case, you're probably reacting to earlier times when a key person was angry in a similar situation. Or do you find yourself suddenly getting sad at some song, movie, TV show, or event when no one else around seems to be having that reaction? Likewise, do you ever find yourself getting angry at something and it just doesn't make sense? Then, of course, there is this big one: Has your spouse ever said "no" to your sexual advances and you felt a huge reaction of anger, resentment, or pain?

All these examples are possibilities of times when older feelings are affecting your current reaction.

A "**trigger**" is the term for any stimulus that brings up much older feelings.

Recently, for example, I was at the funeral of a woman who was the mother of one of my best friends. When they closed the casket I felt intense feelings of sadness and started to cry. Now, I hardly knew this woman. What it touched in me is the death of my own mother, who died when I was three years old. My sadness was really for her.

Over the years I've noticed many things that trigger me into my sadness or anger about the loss of my mother. For example:

- When one of her favorite hymns is played

- When I see a woman who acts or looks like her

- Mother's Day preparations or celebrations

- Certain dates like her birthday or the day she died
- When friends make casual comments about their mother, or even about their parents' wedding anniversary
- When I see a young mother out playing with a little girl
- Anything any woman says to me that suggests rejection or abandonment

And, of course, I can easily be triggered about events other than my mother's death. There are plenty of pockets of pain that can surface for all of us, which will affect our present relationships with those around us. When I'm interacting with my husband, for example, I may be triggered into some old feelings about my father or my sexual abuse perpetrator.

These are only a few illustrations, but they give you some examples of how broad and how trivial these triggers can be. Do you get the idea?

Here's an important principal of being "faithful and true," as Mark Laaser calls it:

Because your woundedness is the pain that drives your addiction, heal your oldest feelings first.
Later feelings will follow, and your healing journey will be more successful.

Your current issues may be the latest evolution or manifestation of wounds that you have felt since childhood. We have a way of repeating old issues, hoping for healing, and we're frustrated when they never seem to go away. This pattern could be true in your current relationships. If you argue with a spouse, friend, or anyone about superficial issues, you will probably stay stuck in repetitive fights, angers, and resentments. It's crucial that you get beneath the obvious problem to the deeper issues, which probably date back to childhood. Those relationships that are able to go deeper are generally the ones that are able to heal.

Eight Specific Trauma Reactions

We all have a variety of ways that we cope with our wounds from the past. Some of us avoid our feelings at all costs. Or we may use addictive activity to medicate those feelings. In his book *The Betrayal Bond*, Patrick Carnes talks about eight possible reactions to our wounds. You may want to read Carnes' book to get a more detailed description of these reactions. I've also discussed them in *No Stones: Women Redeemed from Sexual Shame* (pages 137-140). In addition to your individual reading, it might be good for your L.I.F.E. Recovery Group to spend some time discussing these reactions.

For now, let me list them briefly.

1. **Blocking.** This refers to any behavior or substance that you use to avoid your feelings. Consider how this might be manifested in your life. You've already thought about sexual behaviors, and to some extent, other substances and behaviors. Don't forget those socially acceptable substances like caffeine, in addition to ones like nicotine and alcohol. Make sure you also include what would be considered "positive" behaviors (like work). Sleeping a lot is another example you may not have thought of. The effect of blocking is that you're "numbing" yourself. Mark often refers to this reaction as "going to the land of numb."

2. **Splitting**. The clinical community refers to this reaction as "dissociating." When you split, you "leave." You may be lost in thoughts, daydreaming, or even having fantasies. (Does that sound familiar?) Rape victims are frequently known to leave their bodies and emotionally go to someplace far away. It's like that for some trauma survivors: their minds are removed from current reality.

3. **Abstinence**. This reaction means that you avoid any stimulus that reminds you of the trauma. Some sexual trauma survivors, for example, avoid sex altogether. This pattern is called "sexual anorexia," which is about avoidance. Abstinence can be very specific, such as avoiding certain sexual behaviors. For some, this pattern means avoiding success, or eating, or spending. Spending, for example, reminds them of not having money and thus activates their fear of poverty.

4. **Reactions**. This one is a broad category that refers to any way your mind or your body tells you that you're afraid. You may have dreams that wake you up in the middle of the night. You might experience "flashbacks" or sudden memories that suddenly leap into your mind. Your body may develop aches and pains that don't seem related to any medical condition. Stomachaches, backaches, and headaches are examples. Some chronic pain conditions, like fibromyalgia, could also point to a chronic fear of harm. Any stress-related symptoms could fit into this category.

5. **Repetition**. This reaction means that a person seeks to repeat experiences of trauma for two main possible reasons. First, she might hope for a different outcome. Why do some people seem to keep going back to damaging relationships or situations? It's because of their hope that this time the situation will be resolved or the relationship

will work. The language of AA refers to this pattern as the definition of insanity, when we keep doing the same thing and hoping for a different result. Second, a person might repeat a traumatic situation, but this time she's trying to be the one who is in the power position, rather than the one who's being harmed. There is the mistaken notion that by being in control, the pain of earlier memories will be diminished. This form of trauma repetition is sometimes referred to as the "victim to victimizer" cycle and is often behind offending behaviors.

6. **Bonds**. This pattern describes finding others who will help you play out old situations. When this person "bonds," she gets into relationships with people who remind her in some way of the person(s) who created the original harm. Why do our husbands sometimes remind us of characteristics of our mothers or fathers? That's one example of a trauma bond. Examine your relationships and ask if you aren't seeking to replay old patterns with this person for either of the reasons described in the paragraph above about trauma repetition. In the cartoon strip "Peanuts," for example, why does Charlie Brown keep going back to a spiteful Lucy, who always pulls the football away?

7. **Pleasure**. This trauma reaction is one of the most painful patterns, possibly literally. People who have this pattern find pleasure in pain. Those who get involved with sado-masochistic behavior, for example, find sexual high from painful situations. It could be that they are recreating situations from their past - ones in which they found the only touch or attention they ever received. It could also mean that the excitement and adrenalin or the fear and danger involved get neurochemically programmed in their brain. This woman becomes addicted to the rush of her own neurochemistry in painful or threatening situations.

8. **Shame**. Old wounds create the core belief that "I am a bad and worthless person." People who experience trauma shame don't know how to be happy or content. They find a sense of identity from feeling shameful. They can often play the victim or martyr role.

Don't be frightened by these trauma reactions. With the help of your group and possibly a therapist, you can gain important insights from identifying which reactions apply to you. Understanding them can help you create new behaviors and boundaries that will break these patterns. You don't have to remain shackled to the traumas of the past. You can experience abundant L.I.F.E. that Jesus offers.

Writing Exercise: Your Trauma Reactions

Note in your journal which trauma reactions apply to you. Describe specifically how you experience them.

Fantasy: A Window Into Your Trauma

The final segment of Assignment Three may be the most daunting, but it's possibly the most helpful. Working on this assignment has the best potential for interrupting your sex addiction cycle. It involves understanding your fantasies.

First, an underlying principle:

Fantasies are an attempt to create an ideal world or scenario in which all of our wounds are healed.

Think about it: Fantasies are a key way we try to correct pain from our past. This pain doesn't have to be about sex. *It's pain about who we really are.* Our fantasies may correct our sense of our identity and our importance in the world. In our fantasies we're powerful, successful, and lovable. In our fantasies we get touched, praised, nurtured, and affirmed. We are immensely desirable.

Take romantic fantasies, for example. Don't many of us have those? In our fantasy, we find our Prince Charming and we're adored, cherished, and passionately loved. Mr. Wonderful sweeps us off our feet and caters to our every want and need. These fantasies correct all the disappointments, the losses, and relationship failures of the past.

What about money fantasies? In mine, I have all the money I need for anything. I win the lottery and have magnificent houses, cars, clothes, and jewelry. People are impressed with my success and my wealth.

Now turn to sexual fantasies. What wounds are you correcting in your sexual or relational fantasies? You need to be desired and affirmed. You need to be touched. You need to feel you're admired. In your fantasies, attractive people want you and are dying to be with you. Attentive partners will do anything for you. Or it may simply be that your intimate relationship with your husband isn't as exciting and provocative as you imagined it would be, and your fantasies provide the thrills you long for. On the other hand, the meaning behind your fantasy may be more complicated than that.

Before we go any further, do an exercise: Describe your most common fantasy. Be careful and don't get into the fantasy too far. Don't be graphic or write the great American pornography novel. Be an observer of the events, not a participant. Complete the exercise about the fantasy that you're most likely to play out in your mind. It may be the most recent, or it may be the one you've imagined a thousand or more times over the course of your life. It may have variations, but describe the common elements. Your main objective will be to distill out the theme of the fantasy. Be courageous and honest in describing your fantasy. Remember that your secrets have kept you in bondage. Use the suggested questions as a guide.

Writing Exercise: Your Fantasy

1. Who shows up? Is it one person or more than one? Male or female or both? What do they look like? Is he or she tall, short, fat, skinny, blond, red head, or brunette? Are there other important physical characteristics like broad shoulders or long legs? (Do you get the picture?)

2. How does the main character(s) act? What is his or her emotional nature? Kind, sympathetic, and compassionate? Or harsh, aloof, or abusive? Is the person seductive? Does he or she seem to want you intensely? What is the individual's personality?

3. Where does the fantasy take place? What's the setting, the mood, and the ambience? For example, is it on a mountaintop, in the bedroom, or in front of a fire? Does the setting seem safe or frightening?

4. What is the nature of the sexual activity? Be specific, but you don't need to be detailed. For example, "sexual intercourse" or "oral sex" is descriptive but not graphic. Be fearless as you describe the activity.

IMPORTANT INSTRUCTION: **Read the Safety Guidelines aloud in your L.I.F.E. Recovery Group before anyone shares her fantasy. Emphasize the reminder to avoid sexually explicit language or descriptions.**

NOTE: *Most of you will discover that not all of these four categories are equally important. You may not care who shows up as long as a certain sexual activity takes place. You may not care about the sex particularly as long as a certain kind of person is involved. Maybe the setting is what's most important to you. Our fantasies are as varied as our wounds and our desires and needs.*

Learning From Your Fantasy

Once you have the description of your most common fantasy, the main goal is to determine what it means. *Let me remind you that your fantasy holds a key to your healing.* No matter how debased, horrible, or bizarre your fantasy may seem, there's a *reason* behind it. The first clue to the underlying meaning may surface during this next assignment.

Writing Exercise: Your Themes

> *Write a brief paragraph about the themes you see in your fantasy.*
> *Share them with your group when you explain your fantasy.*

Remember, your fantasy is a window into your trauma. It can be an important messenger about the wounds you need to heal. What does the theme(s) of your fantasy suggest about your needs? Remember the principle: This fantasy could be your attempt to heal the trauma of your abuse or abandonment.

There perhaps are other reasons why you have this fantasy. It could be based on actual life experiences that you found really exciting. It could come from pornography that you've seen. It could simply be the repetition of the adrenalin that was created in thinking it up. My guess is that even if these other explanations are true, the fantasy speaks to the deepest longings of your heart for love and nurture.

Perhaps the person who shows up resembles a person who abandoned you. Maybe he or she has the characteristics of love, nurture, and desire that you long for. The setting could be one in which you feel safe, excited, or stimulated. It might also be some kind of reenactment of previous experiences, even traumatic ones. (Remember the nature of the trauma reactions described earlier). The kind of sexual activity you think about might symbolize ultimate excitement. It might also symbolize ultimate love. Fantasizing about oral sex, for example, may suggest that you're either being totally accepted or that you are totally consuming the essence of your sexual partner. For some women, the fantasy doesn't involve specific sexual activity at all. Instead, the important feature is some kind of emotional connection. What does that suggest about what's missing in your life?

Why is understanding your fantasy so important? *If fantasy is an attempt to heal a part of your spirit, if you try to shut off your fantasy, you'll squelch the voice of your soul.*

Some uninformed counselors, pastors, or recovering people believe the goal is to stop fantasizing. I totally disagree. Fantasies can be your friend, because they provide crucial clues about the direction of your healing journey. They can be a map of the road to freedom.

Recovery isn't merely about stopping addictive behavior. Genuine transformation requires the healing of your spirit. You must give voice to the deepest longing of your soul. If you don't, your soul will find other ways to communicate with you. It craves to be heard, perhaps just as you did when you were a child.

If you can hear that voice of your soul and find healthy ways
to heal the wounds, your fantasies will go away. You won't need them.

Are you listening? Can you identify the deepest desires of your heart? Talk with your L.I.F.E. Recovery Group about better answers to your need for affirmation, praise, touch, nurture, safety, acceptance, and belonging.

As Christians, we know that the main answer to our core longings and needs is a relationship with God through his Son Jesus Christ. You must come to believe that God loves you just as you are. There is no sin that stops Him from loving you. You have no need too great for Him to meet; you have no wound too deep for Him to heal.

Another part of the answer lies in your relationship with other Christians. We all need God "with skin on." One of the richest blessings of being in a L.I.F.E. Recovery Group is the fellowship with other sisters, who can serve as conduits of God's healing touch on your life.

Writing Exercise: Your Desires

Ask God to teach you the meaning of your fantasy and how you can find more ultimate fulfillment in a deepening relationship with Him. Journal about this hunger for God and for safe relationships. Discuss these core longings with your group and/or your therapist.

Congratulations! You've just finished the most difficult emotional assignment in the entire *L.I.F.E. Recovery Guide*. You're well on your way to identifying the root causes that have driven your addiction. You've glimpsed the core desires of your heart. My prayer is that you will begin to find new freedom from old memories, thoughts, and behaviors.

PRINCIPLE TWO

We believe in God, accept the grace offered through His Son Jesus Christ, and surrender our lives and our wills to Him on a daily basis.

Finding the Solution: I Have Only One Option

Assignment Three – Outlining Our Darkness

I invite you to do an imaginative exercise somewhat like you did when you considered your most frequent sexual fantasy. This time, though, you'll be imagining a scene that springs from hope, instead of one that comes from the pain of the past. First, if your description or picture of God (Assignment Two of this Principle) is of an angry or distant Being, recreate (at least in your mind) an image that more accurately portrays God's love and grace.

Now I want you to see yourself interacting with that kind of God. This is the "Abba" God – the intimate "daddy" God. This is the God who would ride you on His shoulders, throw ball with you, listen your stories, and comfort your fears. This is the perfect father. (A good description of this biblical view of God may be found in Sandra Wilson's *Into Abba's Arms* or in many of the writings by Max Lucado.)

Imagine the two of you talking and laughing together. Try to picture some specific activity or conversation. Observe all the details of the setting. Let this scene become real in your mind.

You can be confident that God is truly the loving, caring Abba Father you imagined. It's safe to depend on Him, because He is 100% trustworthy. To surrender to God is to place your life and will into the care of One who is eager to be in relationship with you. God loved you enough that He sent His only Son to die on the cross for your sins.

The connection you've sought through sinful sexual practices is really the longing for intimacy with God. Your passion is to be known and loved and cherished, despite your faults. Only God can fulfill that desire. Intimacy with Him can never be found through pursuit of the flesh.

An important part of your transformation process will be to experience the fathering of your Abba God. Only His love and the grace of Christ can sustain and heal you. All other substitutes are false. And the path to this intimacy with God begins with surrender.

Writing Exercises: Placing Hope in God

---

1. *Write a description of this encounter with God in your journal. Be specific; include as much detail as possible. What did you do? How did God respond? What did you say to each other? Share your image with someone from your L.I.F.E. Recovery Group.*

2. *Compose a statement of surrender to God. (The Third Step Prayer of AA is an example.) Remember, the wording and grammar isn't important. The intent of your heart is what matters. Offer the prayer at your next group meeting or share it with your pastor or accountability partner.*

Two passages of Scripture seem particularly appropriate to this Principle about putting our hope in God and surrendering totally our wills to Him:

"Come to Me, all you who labor and are heavy laden,
and I will give you rest.
Take My yoke upon you and learn from Me,
for I am gentle and lowly in heart,
and you will find rest for your souls.
For My yoke is easy and My burden is light."

(Matthew 11: 28-30)

"If anyone desires to come after Me,
let him deny himself, and take up his cross,
and follow Me.
For whoever desires to save his life will lose it,
and whoever loses his life for My sake
will find it.
For what is a man profited if he gains the whole world,
and loses his own soul?
Or what will a man give in exchange for his soul?"

(Matthew 16: 24-26)

PRINCIPLE THREE

We make a list of our sins and weaknesses and confess those to a person of spiritual authority.

Telling the Truth: I Must Leave the Darkness

Assignment Three - Confessing Our Darkness

This assignment is quite simple but extremely vital to your spiritual recovery. In James 5:16, the brother of Jesus tells us that we should confess our sins to one another. This assignment is your time to make a confession in a formal way. By "formal" I mean in a way that is spiritually significant to you.

Take note that this is Assignment Three of Principle Three. This *L.I.F.E. Recovery Guide* hasn't asked you to do confession sooner because you needed to take the time to carefully consider your life. The timing was also designed to keep you from rushing out and confessing to everyone who came along, which is a temptation for some. These people believe that if they confess and get it over with, everything will be right with their worlds. This kind of shallow confession can feel cathartic and may be dangerous. It's not appropriate to confess to everyone.

Here are several questions to reflect on as you prepare for this assignment:

1. Have you done serious and prayerful work on the first two assignments of Principle Three?

2. Have you looked at all areas of your life, not just the sexual ones?

3. Have you considered your reason for confessing at this time? What do you hope to accomplish? To be instantly forgiven by everyone? To be done with this painful process forever?

I remember a famous evangelist years ago who publicly confessed his sexual sins on his TV show. He cried and lamented, then he quoted a variety of scriptures about God's grace and how we all need to forgive each other. There was something about his presentation and attitude that didn't feel quite right. Not surprisingly, several months later he relapsed with the same sexual behaviors.

For confession to be genuine, it must occur according to these important guidelines:

- Confession is done out of humility, not arrogance.

- Don't confess to anyone whose forgiveness you might be trying to manipulate.

- Don't confess if you expect that this is the one and only time.

- Don't confess if you're just trying to get it over with.

- Don't confess if you're thinking that others will be mad at you if you don't.

- Confession is a genuine act of repentance, not something you do because you got caught.

Pray and mull over these parameters for authentic confession. Then get some feedback from your L.I.F.E. Recovery Group about your motivation and readiness to take this step at this time.

I've always been bothered by the brief and usually collective acts of confession that most of us have done at church services. We might read together something printed in the bulletin, or we might pray silently to God about our sins. Those acts aren't enough.

The Roman Catholics have been better at confession than most Protestant groups. I'm aware of how perfunctory or ritualistic confession may have become for many Catholics. It is, however, a sacrament, a *sacred* act to be done with a person (a priest) of spiritual authority. This principle of spiritual authority is important.

Consider who represents spiritual authority for you. Be careful here and don't automatically assume that it's your current pastor. Maybe you don't have a current pastor, because you don't have a regular church relationship. Maybe you don't like your current pastor.

Take the time to contemplate the idea of spiritual authority. Start with the religious traditions of your youth. Even though you may have converted to a different church body, you may still have a place in your heart that recognizes the spiritual authority of your childhood. I've talked to many people, for example, who have converted from Roman Catholicism to a Protestant denomination. But they still remember the spiritual authority of a priest, and their heart still warms at the thought of hearing words of forgiveness from the mouth of a priest.

Part of your thinking should consider the role of authority in the Church. Do you believe that God calls some to be pastors and evangelists and that they've been given spiritual authority to represent God's grace? Today, who do you say is "my pastor"?

Maybe it's still someone from the past. Possible candidates would be the person who led you to the Lord, a person who discipled or mentored you, a previous pastor, or a respected Bible teacher or Sunday School teacher. It might even be a Christian counselor or possibly the facilitator of your L.I.F.E. Recovery Group.

Writing Exercise

Write the names of a handful of people who represent spiritual authority to you. _____ _____ _____

Now, is it possible to schedule an appointment with someone from your list to go over all the work you've done in Principle Three? These meetings sometimes take hours because there's so much to say, so you need to be sure the person has enough time available to hear you out.

After you've scheduled this appointment, write down the time in your journal. Then report this meeting to your L.I.F.E. group, and ask the members to hold you accountable for keeping it. If it's not possible to meet with the first person on your list, keep going until you find someone who is available. Pray that the Lord will lead you to the right "priest."

My prayer is that you'll have a powerful encounter with the marvelous grace of God during this time of confession. I hope you'll find a listener who will be the ears and voice that reminds you of God's love and forgiveness.

Follow-up Writing

After you've had this time of confession, journal about what it was like. You might write just a few sentences or paragraphs, or it may be longer. But it should be a definite entry in your journal that records this spiritual milestone.

As a final exercise, at your next L.I.F.E. Recovery Group use some time during check in to report on your experience of confession. You might also, at some point, agree to be the person who does the talk on Principle Three for the appropriate meeting. Sharing what AA calls your "experience, strength, and hope" about confession would be a wonderful experience for you and a blessing to your sisters.

PRINCIPLE FOUR

We seek accountability and to build our character as children of God.

Growing in Transformation: I Mature in Character

Assignment Three – Cultivating Our Character

Principle Four is about growing in transformation and maturing in character. This assignment focuses on how we *cultivate* our character. Fortunately, we have a detailed description of a mature character: the fruits of the Spirit that Paul describes in Galatians 5. These godly fruits are love, joy, peace, patience, kindness, goodness, faithfulness, gentleness and self-control. Wouldn't we all like to be more like that in character? Again, modeling ourselves after these qualities will be a lifetime journey. Hopefully, as you continue your journey of healing, you'll develop self-control more and more.

One of the keys to the other qualities of character is the ability to be empathetic. **Empathy** is that ability to put yourself in the place of someone else and to completely understand what he or she is going through. Do you begin to see that your addiction has given you an opportunity to be more empathetic? You're beginning to understand your wounds, your pain, your loneliness, your anger, and your fear. This understanding will help you better understand those feelings in others. You'll be able to listen to their stories and understand their pain. You'll be more patient, kind, good, gentle, and peaceful. This change in character comes from your own humility.

This assignment is one piece in your ongoing journey to develop empathy. *Selfishness, of course, is the enemy of empathy.* Since most of us are turned off by the selfishness of others, why are we so often selfish? Mark Laaser suggests this principle:

Selfishness is equal to unhealed wounds.

Selfish people are those who feel that their needs haven't been met. Selfish people are also those who think only *they* can meet their own needs. This belief is an aspect of the original sin, "I control my life; I don't trust God to do it." As you continue to work this program, you'll discover more and more that only God can meet your needs. You'll also find some of your desires are being met through safe, intimate relationships with others. You should become less selfish as you learn that there are healthy ways to get what you need.

Empathy for Others

Empathy begins when you discover that others are just as wounded as you are. One of the great tasks of recovery is to understand that you're not alone in your wounds. As you listen to others in your L.I.F.E. Recovery Group, the universality of pain should become clear. As a way of aiding that process, Assignment Three asks you to do some rather strange things.

Writing Exercise: Cultivating Empathy

1.   First, interview one of your accountability partners about the wounds she's experienced. Make a list of these wounds in your journal. (Obviously, ask her permission first. It's probably best to not identify her by name.)

2.   Now, pick a member of your family. It may be your husband, a sibling, cousin, uncle or aunt, or anyone else you feel safe with. If that safe person isn't your husband yet, then use someone else. (This person should have done some reflecting about his or her own life journey. Don't seek to educate this person or convince her of any wounds she hasn't accepted or understood.) Interview this person about the wounds she's discovered about herself, and write in your journal about what you learned in this interview.

Let's continue with a rather dangerous assignment by imagining your last acting out partner. It may be a person in a pornographic picture or it may be someone you were with physically. It may be a person you lusted after. *NOTE: Even if you have the opportunity to interview this person, <u>don't</u>.*

I want you to simply imagine what it might have been like for this person growing up. Let me help you. For example, do you know that the vast majority of women who pose for pornography were sexually abused as little girls? The same would be true for your average prostitute, both female and male. What's the life history of your last affair partner? In what ways was he wounded as a child? Remember, all of these people are someone's daughter or son, someone's sibling, and perhaps someone's husband or wife. Do you see what I mean?

Writing Exercise

In your journal, write a few paragraphs that tell the life story of the acting out partner you chose. What do you think it was like for this person as a child? What pain or life challenges has he or she endured?

162

One of the basic truths about sexual acting out is that you have to objectify that person - that is, imagine him or her as an object - to diminish any feelings of guilt or discomfort that you might otherwise have. When you view your sexual partners as wounded human beings, you gain empathy for their pain, and it's much harder to objectify them.

Affirming Others

Now, let's work on cultivating character in another direction. How are you in being affirming and encouraging? Many of us, since we were abandoned of those positive strokes ourselves, have a hard time being that way with others, particularly those whom we really love.

You might have to diligently practice this one. Make a conscious effort to be affirming and encouraging of your sisters in your L.I.F.E. Recovery Group. When you give any feedback to someone who has shared, start with an affirmation. Be encouraging before, during, and after meetings.

Now, consider those around you whom you love. Who do you suspect is really starved for affirmation and encouragement? Maybe it's your spouse. Remember that he might not be acting like he needs encouragement because he's so angry or withdrawn. If you have children, they probably need affirmation.

Writing Exercise: Affirmation

> *Make a commitment to affirm someone close to you every day. Note in your journal what you did and how the person reacted.*

Reflect back on a person who was affirming and encouraging in your life. It may not be the person whom you hoped it would be, like your mom or dad. Do you remember how kind and generous and patient and loving that person was to you? Wouldn't you like to offer those gifts to someone else?

I've seen some miraculous changes in other people when I've simply taken the time to affirm them. Imagine the smile on someone's face who might delight in your encouraging words.

You'll find that if you carry out these assignments, your character will improve. You'll become more patient, kind, gentle, and self-controlled. And the reason? It is, of course, your ability to be empathetic. Do you see how important it is to cultivate your character in this area?

NOTE: If you find you have a hard time affirming others, go back to the anger section and continue to work on your core woundedness. Remember that there is no shame in talking to a pastor, counselor, or trusted friend.

Exercise from Scripture

Study two separate but related scriptures and consider the words of Christ:

Luke 6: 27-49
Matthew 7: 1-12

Write in your journal your thoughts about these two teachings.

Finally, remember again that character formation is a lifetime journey. Affirm yourself for finally thinking about these things and taking them seriously.

Principle Five

We explore the damage we have done, accept responsibility, and make amends for our wrongs.

Demonstrating Real Change: I Accept Responsibility

Principle Five marks a turning point in your journey of transformation. Here's a review of your work to this point as guided by the first four Principles: You admit the unmanageability of your life because of sexual sin and your inability to solve the problem on your own. Next, you choose to surrender totally to Christ and to seek God's will for your life on a daily basis. You inventory your history with complete honesty and reveal the truth through specific confession to another person. Then you address your flaws and inadequacies of character by entering into relationships of accountability.

These first four Principles are vital in forming the foundation for genuine, lasting change. You examine the depth of your sinful nature and your need for God. You take the huge steps of telling the truth and asking for help.

The journey this far, though, is also largely self-focused. These examinations and confessions and submission to accountability require great introspection. You're looking inward and exploring your own life, behavior, mind and heart.

Principle Five expands your investigation. It challenges you to look outside of yourself and consider the ways your sexual sin has impacted others. You admit that you're not isolated in your sin and that it has repercussions for others. People in your life are affected by your addiction. Your actions have caused pain for many, probably more than you'd like to think. In a variety of ways, your behavior and character flaws have harmed others. The process of Principle Five begins with a thorough assessment of the damage caused by your sexual sin, its consequences and your character flaws. Like Nehemiah, you venture outside yourself to survey the damage that exists in your environment. You observe the fallout of your life. You catalog the pain you've caused for others. You look unflinchingly at the harm you've brought about.

Assignment Three - Living Amends

Assignments One and Two of Principle Five led you through a process of identifying those you've harmed and creating specific plans for making amends. Now, in Assignment Three, you have the opportunity to demonstrate real change. By taking action in making amends, you will show in overt ways the revolutions that are happening within your heart. For those around you, it may be the first clear example of your "walking the walk" of transformation.

Making Specific Amends

This assignment considers two broad ways of making amends. First, we'll examine taking **specific actions**, whether directly or indirectly, of making restitution. Making indirect amends is less complicated. After getting feedback from your group, simply take the action of vicarious restitution. Do it quietly, without fanfare or attempts to draw attention to yourself.

Making **direct amends** is more risky. Be aware of these **guidelines** about your conversation with someone you've harmed:

- <u>State the reason you want to talk to this person</u>. Remember, you've probably hurt this individual in some deep way, and he or she may be wary about talking with you. If you make a specific appointment to meet, explain then why you want to talk. If you haven't contacted someone on your list, but God provides an unexpected opportunity for an impromptu conversation, state in the beginning your desire to express your sorrow at the harm you've caused.

- <u>Then state clearly how you've hurt this person.</u> Be specific. General apologies are lame. Instead of "I'm sorry I hurt you," say "I know it was painful when I forgot your birthday because I was absorbed in my sexual sin. I apologize." Be sure to say the actual words, *"I'm sorry and I apologize."* The mind-set of remorse is too important to let it be merely understood. I believe it's better, though, to avoid asking for forgiveness. It's too easy to be manipulative with a request for forgiveness. If the person extends forgiveness, that's great. But that choice is his or hers and should be made freely without prompting from you. Simply express your sorrow for the pain you've caused and let go of the outcome. You are powerless over the person's reaction.

- <u>Explain your intention to behave differently and any plan of restitution you'd like to make for the harm you've caused this person.</u> Again, be specific about what you'd like to do to right the wrong.

- <u>Listen to the individual's reaction.</u> He or she may express anger or hurt at what you've done. Be patient and non-defensive. Agree with the harm you've caused and be empathetic to the person's pain.

166

- <u>Thank the person for listening to your apology and for expressing his or her thoughts or feelings.</u>

Don't expect any certain reaction or outcome when you try to make specific amends. Some people won't understand what you're doing and may brush you off. Others may still be too angry to hear you out. Perhaps more will accept your apology. The individual's reaction isn't the issue. *Your willingness to humbly accept responsibility is the key point.* Remember the teaching in I Peter 5: 6: "Humble yourselves … under God's mighty hand, that He may lift you up in due time." Making amends is as much for you as it is for those you've harmed. It further releases your burden of shame and deepens your trust in God to take care of the outcome when you submit your will to Him.

Practicing Living Amends

The life-long challenge and task of recovery is to live differently, not only in your sexual behavior, but in all areas of your life. By thought, word and deed, an addict must daily observe the principles of being faithful and true. In recovery terms, this kind of practice is called "living amends." In every situation you make the decisions, to the best of your ability, that are beneficial instead of harmful.

A first area of living amends is obviously to maintain sexual sobriety. Without sexual integrity, no other progress is possible. (I'll discuss this concept at length in Principle Six.) Remember the caution that was part of the final assignment of Principle One: This period of time during your second six months of sobriety is a dangerous time for relapse. It's easy to get lax about your recovery efforts. I want to remind you of one important tool of working your program. *Boundaries remain critical to your sexual sobriety.* Review your work on boundaries from Principle One. Are you practicing good boundaries in the physical area? Mental? Emotional? Spiritual? Relational? Don't let down your guard.

A second major part of practicing living amends is following the Golden Rule: treating others the way you'd like to be treated. This goal requires maturity and self-sacrifice. It doesn't come naturally, especially to addicts who have a long history of focusing on their own gratification. A key way this objective relates to Principle Five is in learning to forgive others, just as you hoped they would forgive you when you offered your amends.

Your work this far through this text and with your L.I.F.E. Recovery Group has put you in touch with some profound areas of your own woundedness. You've identified ways you've been deeply hurt by others, perhaps even some in your own family. You've allowed yourself to feel your feelings of loss, grief, hurt, anger, sadness and loneliness. You understand the ways you've been abused or abandoned.

Principle Five challenges you to forgive those who have harmed you, as well as to humbly make amends to those you have harmed. For some of us, this undertaking is more difficult. Maybe you'd like to nurse your resentments a little longer. Perhaps you've become comfortable in your victim role. Holding on to a grudge lets you ignore any part you may have contributed to the relationship problems.

A clear sign of a changed life course is when you're willing to let go of the dues others owe you. Whether or not the offender expresses sorrow at the pain he or she has caused, you choose to forgive and move forward. You allow God to be the judge and the punisher for wrongs. Paul issues this challenge:

> *"Do not repay anyone evil for evil.... If it is possible, as far as it depends on you, live at peace with everyone. Do not take revenge, my friends, but leave room for God's wrath, for it is written, 'It is mine to avenge; I will repay,' says the Lord. On the contrary: 'If your enemy is hungry, feed him; if he is thirsty, give him something to drink....' Do not be overcome by evil, but overcome evil with good."* (Romans 12: 17-21)

Don't be discouraged by how difficult it is to make amends to others and to extend grace to others. This will be a life-long process as you grow in your relationship with a forgiving God. You won't do either of these recovery tasks perfectly. Sometimes you won't have the maturity or judgment to even try. Because you're human, you will continue to cause harm occasionally.

Remember our Lord's promise: *"My grace is sufficient for you, for my power is made perfect in weakness."* (2 Corinthians 12: 9)

Exercise: Your Tasks

Take two specific actions:

    1. Make one direct amends to someone you've harmed

    2. Make one form of indirect amends

Record what you did in your journal, along with how you felt. Be prepared to share your actions and feelings with your L.I.F.E. Recovery Group.

Share the names and situations with your sponsor. Pray together for willingness and help in letting go of your right to avenge the wrongs you've suffered.

Five People I Need to Forgive:

1. _____

2. _____

3. _____

4. _____

5. _____

Ask your group for affirmations about how far you've come in your journey of Living In Freedom Everyday.

Principle Six

In fellowship with others we develop honest, intimate relationships, where we celebrate our progress and continue to address our weaknesses.

Living in Fellowship: I Cannot Succeed Alone

Congratulations on getting this far in your journey to maintain integrity in your sexual behavior and relationships. I know it's taken courage, perseverance and commitment. In many ways it may have been harder than you anticipated. You've experienced many feelings that may be new to you. You've had to humble yourself in admitting the full truth about your history, your thoughts and your offenses. But with God's help, you've done it. You've told your story of sexual sin. You've decided you want to get well and have surrendered your life to Christ. You've accepted accountability from a sponsor and perhaps have begun working with a counselor. You're willing to make amends to those you have harmed. I pray you're beginning to have a deeper sense of God's power and presence in your life.

Principle Six guides you into a way of living that involves genuine connection with others, instead of the isolation you've probably known. The foundation for this work comes from one of Mark Laaser's core teaching principles:

Fellowship is equal to freedom from lust.

It's probably hard for you to believe this promise. You may have been alone for years as you've hidden your sexual secrets from others. You've never known the joy of a supportive community. Your shame kept you from connecting with others, while it continued to fuel your lust and sexual sin. (You also probably can't imagine a life free from fantasy and lust, which have felt like your constant companions for as long as you can remember.) Principle Six offers a path out of your isolation, which in turn, is the road to sexual integrity.

Hopefully, you're already enjoying some of the benefits of fellowship through your L.I.F.E. Recovery Group. You're bonding with other Christian women who've faced similar struggles and seek to live in sexual freedom and purity. You're beginning to experience both the grace of God and the grace of other Christians who will love you despite your mistakes.

Assignment Three – Growing In Spirituality

The main activity of this assignment is a matter of "**conversion**." No, it's probably not what you're thinking. I don't mean the kind of conversion that changes a person from a non-Christian to a Christian. You've hopefully already done that. The conversion I'm proposing is about converting all the energy you used to pursue *sex* into energy that you use to pursue *God.*

You know, of course, that the key to this conversion will be **discipline** – an ongoing discipline necessary to make ongoing change in your life. Note how the word "discipline" is from the same root word as "disciple." This word is rarely used in the Old Testament, but in the New Testament, it's used to refer to a follower of Jesus. Does that description fit you? If so, you must be a woman of discipline.

You already have some of the characteristics of a disciple. For example, you have the *energy* to follow Christ. Think again of how much energy you spent being a follower of sex and relationships. (If you can't remember, go back and review Principle One.) If you can't seem to find the energy for a spiritual walk, you may be experiencing some level of shame and depression.

You have the *plan* to follow Christ. Do you remember the category of ritual in the cycle of addiction? Ritual isn't a bad word; it can be a spiritual one. You'll need rituals to pursue your spiritual path.

For this assignment you'll also need "**enthusiasm**." Enthusiasm is a Greek word that literally means that God, "Theos," is in us. *God is in you.* Did you know that?

Read the entire fifteenth chapter of the Gospel of John. Jesus says that He will be in you if you are in Him. He says a lot of other things, doesn't He? He describes the vine and the branches and how the Master Gardner prunes the branches that don't produce fruit. Are you feeling rather pruned? As you learn to abide in Christ, you'll draw nourishment from Him, and you'll bear more fruit.

In Assignment One of Principle Six, you started keeping a daily inventory. One of the categories you were asked to assess was spirituality. In this assignment, I want you to be much more aggressive in your thinking about this area.

Sometimes when we think about spiritual discipline, we mean that we need to have a "quiet time." My experience suggests that many addicts aren't very good at that practice. We're impatient by nature and we don't like doing anything "quietly." For the restless among us, increasing our spirituality may be a matter of doing something more active, such as going somewhere to participate in Bible study or corporate prayer or corporate meditation. It may mean going to concerts or Christian seminars. It may be putting a cassette or CD into your car stereo and listening to praise music or inspirational teaching while you're driving. (We addicts like to multi-task.) There are also many different kinds of workbooks that might help you grow in spiritual discipline. I think of Henry Blackaby's *Experiencing God*, for example. Be creative in planning how you can better connect with God, just as you were creative in your addiction.

Another way of describing what we're after is "**quest**." We're on a religious quest to get closer to God. For some, the quest may involve many active behaviors designed to help find Him. I have known women, for example, who actually travel to places of religious significance, like the Holy Lands, as a way of "experiencing God." This kind of quest may not be something that many of you can afford, but it's an example of something active. A spiritual retreat or dedicated time away from your daily responsibilities is another activity that could be part of a spiritual quest.

For some of us, discipline or quest may mean doing some act of service. It could be working in the soup kitchen, volunteering at church, visiting in the nursing home, or planning a mission trip. We might volunteer for work or participate in a church activity. We might teach a Sunday School class. (There's nothing quite like teaching to help you study yourself.)

Are you getting the idea? To be spiritually disciplined, you need to *do* something. It will probably be something you've never done before – perhaps even a practice far outside your comfort zone. You may need encouragement to get it done, which you can request from your L.I.F.E. Recovery Group.

In some church traditions there's a role for "spiritual director," who is one who directs your prayer life, Bible study, and meditations. Has there ever been such a person in your life? In this recovery program, you might originally think of your sponsor as one who directs you in spiritual discipline. In this assignment, you may want to think of another person who can fill this role.

I encourage you to think "outside the box." Your spiritual director may not be from your own tradition or denomination. The key to this role of "spiritual director" is to hold you accountable to those things that you have agreed to do. Your pastor may suggest some women in your church who are willing to take on such a role.

Maybe you don't have a regular church where you attend. It could be time to "shop" for one until you discover the fellowship where you feel both comfortable and challenged.

Finally, here is one last thought. In John 15, Jesus says that there is no greater gift than to lay down your life for another. Addicts are terrible at practicing self-sacrifice. *Our lust has been selfish*. As we grow in spirituality, we'll be transformed into *selflessness*. Think about the theme of sacrifice as you consider what you should do to have more discipline. Whatever the activity, it should involve some sacrifice of your time, energy, resources, or money.

Writing Exercises: Growing in Spirituality

1.   *Write the name of a person(s) who will hold you accountable to having more spiritual discipline in your life.*

2.   *What is one act of service you're willing to do?*

3.   *Name a section of Scripture you commit to studying.*

4.   *Who is a spiritual teacher you enjoy? What books are you reading or tapes are you listening to?*

5.   *What is your favorite kind of spiritual music?*

6.   *If you're participating in a Bible study or similar class, note that.*

7.   *Have you attended any workshops or seminars recently?*

8.   *Where are you attending worship services? Does this church feel like home? Why or why not?*

These are just some suggestions to help you begin practicing spiritual disciplines. Remember, there's no such thing as the perfect spiritual program. This growth is a journey for life. If you've accepted Christ as your savior, you've already received salvation, so spiritual discipline isn't about your effort to win favor with God. It's about your time with God and your attempt to know Him more intimately.

God's blessings to you in this quest.

PRINCIPLE SEVEN

As we live in sexual integrity, we carry the message of Christ's healing to those who still struggle, and we pursue a vision of God's purpose for our lives.

Finding a Purpose: I Have a Vision

Assignment Three: Discovering Your Vision

Having a vision is a familiar Biblical concept. Both the Old and New Testaments recount the stories of countless people who acted according to their visions. Today, a "vision" is a popular term to describe an inspiring or motivating mental image of the future.

In Assignment Three, you'll work on having that kind of positive mental image of where God wants you to go. Do you remember the earlier work around understanding your fantasies that was part of Principle One? I expressed my hope that you'd be able to replace the fantasies in your life with a vision.

Here's the comparison:

> *A **fantasy** is an image of a preferred future in which all of your wounds are healed.*

> *A **vision** is an image of a preferred future in which you pursue God's plan for your life.*

From your work in Assignment Two of this Principle, "Sharing Your Pain," you saw how your wounds can be your guides - your teachers - about connecting with God and with others. Your wounds may also become your strengths, in that you're a stronger person for having gone through your experiences in life.

The first task of this assignment is to figure out how you become a person of vision.

First, you must discover and accept your true gifts. You might be surprised to find that for years you've been pursuing what others identified as your gifts - others like your parents. They may or may not have had your best interests at heart. Reflect on the messages your family gave you about what you were supposed to do in life. If all the women in your family were stay-at-home mothers, for example, you may have been pressured (however subtly) to make the same choice. In an opposite vein, if your family was known for generation after generation of doctors, it might have been assumed you'd follow that tradition. Just like some families pass along one or more family names from parent to child, others pass a family vocation. Some religious families direct their children, especially sons, into the ministry. One of my pastor friends says, "I was ordained by my mother and not by God."

Think of your family's messages, its modeling and its values. How were you encouraged or discouraged? What was your role(s) in your family? Were some jobs or careers valued more than others?

Writing Exercise:
Your Family's Mission for You

> *Write the "mission statement" you*
> *internalized from your family.*

For example, mine would be simple. My mission as defined by my family was that I would either teach or be a preacher's wife.

It *is* possible for others to encourage you about your true gifts. First, think of those people in your life who were truly affirming and positive. Maybe it was a teacher, a coach, a pastor, or a friend. These supporters believed in you and encouraged your interests. What skills, talents, and abilities did they affirm in you?

Writing Exercise: Your Encouragers

> *Write the names of supportive people and their affirmations:*
>
> _____   _____
>
> _____   _____
>
> _____   _____
>
> _____   _____

Now, reflect on those times when you've felt truly passionate about what you were doing. These will be times when you're "in the zone" and are certain you're doing exactly the right thing. What do you relish? What brings you a sense of fulfillment? What do you do that light others' faces with joy? For what things have others thanked you?

Writing Exercise: Your Passions

> ***Describe some of the times you felt passionate, energetic, and fulfilled. What were you doing? How did others respond? What were the results?***

Next, reflect on your education and your life experiences. What's been your training? What jobs have you held? Volunteer work you've done? Hobbies? Sports?

Writing Exercise: Your Experience

> ***Prepare or review your "resume" of education, employment, hobbies, and critical life experiences.***

Finally, and this is a hard one, reflect again on what you've learned through painful experiences in your life, including the ones related to your sex addiction. Pain can be a great teacher and guide. God often speaks through hardship. James 1:2 says, *"Count it all joy when you experience various trials, for you know that the testing of your faith produces steadfastness."*

Writing Exercise: Your Lessons

> ***Make a list of all the lessons you've learned through your own pain. Remember, this pain could be about loss, failure, hardship, or crisis.***

You now have several lists and sets of reflections. Read back over them until a picture emerges of your true gifts.

If you've never seen the movie *Chariots of Fire* you might want to rent it. It's a wonderful comparison of two men who pursue their gifts and talents for two different reasons. The main characters in this true story are Eric Liddel and Harold Abrahams, who each are preparing for the 1924 Olympic Games. Both are fast and gifted runners. They're the best two runners in the United Kingdom in the hundred-meter dash, and they both have a dream of winning the Olympic gold medal.

Harold Abrahams is the son of a Jewish businessman. He knows his family has never been fully accepted in English society, and he longs to be accepted. The pain of ethnic prejudice burns inside him and fuels his anger. He concludes that the way to be accepted is to be the world's fastest man and to "run all of his opponents into the ground." He even hires a coach and trains incessantly. Harold Abrahams does win the gold medal in the hundred-meter dash, but the end of the movie shows that it doesn't bring him joy. The accomplishment he'd dreamed about is almost a disappointment.

Eric Liddel is the son of missionaries to China. He's back in Scotland studying to be in ministry and to go back to China himself as a missionary. Eric Liddel knows that his athletic gift is from God. His sister, though, grows concerned that his athletic training for the Olympics is distracting him from his "true" work of studying and preparing to return to China. In a powerful scene, Eric takes his sister out on the hills overlooking Edinburgh, Scotland, and he says, "Jenny, I know that the Lord made me for China, but He also made me fast. *And when I run, I feel God's pleasure.*"

During the Olympic games, Eric Liddel refuses to run the hundred-meter dash because one of the qualifying races is scheduled on a Sunday. He switches to the four hundred-meter dash, instead, and he wins the gold medal. He's elated and knows a true sense of joy.
An interesting detail accurately depicted in *Chariots of Fire* is Eric's unusual running style. In the middle of the race, he would throw back his head and close his eyes. He literally couldn't see where he was going. Eric was a man running with God's help. He understood that when God was in control, he didn't need to see where he was going.

What are you doing when you feel God's pleasure - when you don't need to see where you're going? Bill Hybels of Willow Creek Church says that Christians will know they hear the voice of the Holy Spirit by the joy and excitement they feel about what they're thinking or doing.

Writing Exercise: God's Pleasure

> *Make a list of times when you've felt that you were doing something that brought you pure joy – when you could feel "God's pleasure."*

You now have some lists to think and pray about. They encompass your own perception and the perception of others about your talents and gifts. How does this information match up with the expectations you brought from your family of origin? How does it match with what you're currently doing? Don't just think about these questions vocationally, but in the totality of your life.

Consider your work in Principle Four around developing character traits, which was based on the fruits of the Spirit described in Galatians 5. What do you think determines character? Is it a matter of pure will power or is it a matter of **vision**? Think about it this way. You know that your fantasy life drove your behaviors for years, which led you into traits of character that resulted in despair. *Fantasy is actually a form of a vision*, because it's a mental image of an outcome you desire. If that kind of vision is capable of driving behavior and of driving character, wouldn't you also think that a godly vision would drive behavior and character?

My friend and colleague in ministry, Eli Machen, is fond of talking about buzzards. Much to our distaste, buzzards have a huge appetite for dead animals. God made them that way. He also gave them the sight (or vision capability) to see dead animals miles away from hundreds of feet in the air. Because of their vision, these birds can fly around and see things that we don't see. *Buzzards have a buzzard's character and behavior.* And they teach us an important lesson:

Appetite can drive a vision.

What is your appetite? Remember the story in John 4 of Jesus' encounter with the woman at the well of Samaria. She was thirsty for "living water," but she confused it with relationships with men. Her "appetite" for connecting with men drove her into five marriages and a sixth live-in partner.

What, again, are you thirsty for? In your old life, you were thirsty for sex or a romantic relationship. Some of that is God-given instinctual biology. That appetite drives you to be attracted to men and to produce children. Spiritually, however, we also have an appetite for God. Our problem as sex addicts is that we've confused these two appetites. <u>We've merged our appetite for God with our appetite for sex.</u> Women and men both make this mistake. The great English writer G. K. Chesterton wrote, "A man who knocks at the door of a brothel is looking for God."

We've been thirsty for love, nurture, touch, affirmation, and fellowship. We've thought that we could get these normal desires met through sex, but we've been wrong. (For some of us, nearly dead wrong.) <u>We can only get these things from God.</u> This confused appetite has driven our character and our behavior: We've had a sex addict's behavior born from a flawed character created by a faulty appetite. It's time to get reoriented.

A vision pursues your appetite for God. If you allow yourself to see that truth, it will drive your character and your behavior. It will inform your discipline.

Imagine what it would be like to pursue God with the same energy you've pursued sex.

The next step in understanding your vision is to understand the legacy you hope to create. A legacy is how you'll be remembered and the influence you'll leave on others after you die. Here are some questions to consider, assuming you die before some important people in your life:

1. How would you like your husband to remember you? What will he say about you after you're gone?

2. How also would you like your children to remember you? What will they say about mom at future family gatherings? What stories will they tell about you, your character, and your behavior?

3. Who else will remember you when you die? Who'll want to attend your funeral and why will they want to be there? What will be said at your memorial service? What will be highlighted in your obituary?

4. What contributions and acts of service will you be remembered for?

Writing Exercise: Your Legacy

> *Journal your answers to the questions above. Humbly ask God to show you the truth about your current legacy. If you doubt your ability to see yourself clearly, ask a trusted friend to share her honest impressions.*

Tough questions, aren't they? I suggest that if you can answer them courageously, you'll have a vision of what your true heart desires. Strangely enough, I believe it will be consistent with what God desires for you, too.

When you've worked through all of the suggested writing exercises, you're ready for the last part of this assignment: articulating your personal vision.

Writing Exercise: Your Vision

> **Write in your journal a concise declaration that outlines your vision or mission statement. This description shouldn't be long - just a sentence or two and not more**

As an example, here is mine: "With God's help, I will comfort others as I have been comforted, by teaching, writing, speaking, and counseling about healthy families and sexual integrity."

This brief statement incorporates my gifts, talents, and passion, and expresses what brings me joy. It also describes what I'd like to be remembered for after I'm gone.

Women of integrity are women of vision. They know where they're going and what they want to do. They follow their passions with purity and fervor. If you continue to develop and honor your vision, you'll find that your behaviors will follow. Remember, again, how your sexual and relationship behaviors followed your fantasies. As you're transformed into the woman God intends you to be, your vision will direct your decisions.

Before you finish, go back and look at Mark Laaser's healthy cycle that's presented in Principle Six, Assignment Two. It shows the progression from connection with God and His family, to vision, to healthy disciplines, to healthy choices, to joy. My guess is that you've changed a great deal already. My expectation is that the integrity of your behavior and relationships blesses you with serenity and joy. And my ongoing prayer is that you'll continue to grow in strength and faith as you allow God to transform you into a woman who lives in freedom everyday.

TYING IT ALL TOGETHER:

TRANSFORMATION PRINCIPLES FROM NEHEMIAH

The book of Nehemiah is perhaps less familiar and less frequently studied than many of the other books of the Old Testament. To overlook this book, however, is to miss some of the richest material in the Bible. The teaching hidden in Nehemiah is highly applicable to our journey of living in freedom every day. Indeed, it's a great summary of much of this entire *L.I.F.E. Recovery Guide*. Groups may want to discuss one of these principles at every meeting, or at least at selected meetings.

Several years ago Mark Laaser heard a colleague teach from the book of Nehemiah, and he expanded on those initial thoughts to formulate these eighteen principles. I've adapted them further for women, preferring to go beyond Mark's ideas about "**accountability**" to include broader thoughts about the entire process of **transformation**. As you consider these teachings, I encourage you to seek God's wisdom about how you can act responsibly and courageously to defend against Satan's attacks on your sobriety and your journey of living in freedom everyday.

The story of Nehemiah takes place during a time when the Babylonians had defeated Israel. The city of Jerusalem and the temple of God had been destroyed. Many Jews had been taken back to Babylon to work as slaves. Nehemiah was one of these captives. He apparently had distinguished himself as responsible and trustworthy, because he'd been given an important job: the cupbearer to the Babylonian king, Artaxerxes. The cupbearer was required to taste all of the king's food and drink to make sure that someone wasn't trying to poison him. It was a potentially dangerous job, but at least Nehemiah's living conditions were vastly superior to his fellow slaves.' He got to hang out with the king in the throne room and partake of the finest food in the land. Yet Nehemiah was constantly mindful of his dependence on God and of the devastation of God's holy land.

With this background in mind, consider the following principles from the book of Nehemiah. These 18 principles tie together the process of transformation which is outlined in this *L.I.F.E. Recovery Guide*.

NEHEMIAH:
TRANSFORMATION PRINCIPLES

1. Transformation begins with humility.

2. Transformation depends on honest confession about your situation.

3. Transformation involves asking for help and stating your needs.

4. The journey of healing is never traveled alone.

5. The process of transformation assumes that the enemy wants to defeat us, especially when we start trying to do the right thing.

6. In the face of overwhelming damage and discouragement, rebuilding may be a matter of just getting started.

7. Being transformed requires getting the garbage out of your life.

8. Transformation begins at home.

9. Transformation requires preparing ahead of time for the attacks that will come.

10. Transformation means guarding the weakest places where you're most vulnerable.

11. Accountability is always with a group, not just with one person.

12. Our motivation for transformation should be selfless.

13. Transformation means building as well as defending.

14. Transformation means putting positive things into your life.

15. Transformation is an on-going, lifelong process, but God provides sustaining energy.

16. When tempted, remain committed to transformation without wavering.

17. Transformation targets you for rumors and personal attacks.

18. Transformation results in a willingness to sacrifice even your own life.

Nehemiah Principle One:

Accountability begins with humility.

In the beginning of the book, one of Nehemiah's brothers, Hanani, comes with other men to tell about the destruction of Jerusalem. You might expect that if Nehemiah were to be a great leader, he'd jump up with a plan to do something about this problem. As you read the story, however, you see that when he heard this news, Nehemiah sat down and wept (Neh. 1:4).

In Principle Two of the seven principles of L.I.F.E., you were challenged about your willingness to find sobriety from addiction and sin. Willingness is about humility. It's about knowing that we can't control our own lives. It's about knowing that we need God. Nehemiah is humble with a humility that comes from his great sadness.

You, also, may find humility in your sadness as you consider the destructive nature of your sins. Sadness over your current state is the beginning of transformation. Humility reminds you that you can only get well with the help of God. Those who are broken know they need help. Accountability can only begin when we know that we need help and that we can't do it alone. The basic lesson from the first chapter of Nehemiah is that if you aren't willing to depend on God instead of relying on yourself, you won't find healing.

The rest of chapter one is Nehemiah's prayer to God. He first confesses that the Jews have behaved wickedly. (Remember the work you completed in Principle Three about confession.) The second part of the prayer asks God to restore the Jews to their home. Confessional prayer is the first response of a humble heart. After your confession of humility, ask God to restore you by His grace.

Nehemiah Principle Two:

Accountability depends on honest confession about your situation and repentance.

In the opening of chapter two, Nehemiah still doesn't have a plan. He is still sad. The king, who apparently was quite discerning, asks Nehemiah why he looks so sad and then gives his own diagnosis, recognizing, "This can only be sadness of heart." Nehemiah honestly replies, "Why shouldn't I look so sad when the city where my fathers are buried lies in ruins and its gates have been destroyed by fire?" (Neh. 2:4) The account continues with Nehemiah's admission, "I was very much afraid."

Our journey begins when we honestly admit the condition of our lives. As long as we hide our situation and deny our feelings, we'll remain captives of the enemy. In my experience, what we are not so good at in the church is having opportunities to confess to spiritual authority. I'm not talking about some printed confession in the Sunday bulletin. No, face to face confession, I believe, is much more important. We learn a lot about confession and willingness to ask for help in our families. When we think we don't need help, we often lie to others who ask us how we are doing and we say, "fine," for most of us, most of the time that's just not true. When we don't share our feelings with those we love and those we want to be in relationship with, it keeps us isolated and even distant. This isolation creates loneliness, a feeling that most of us really don't like talking about. The bottom line is how can we be accountable to anyone or any group if we don't know how to share our feelings?

Along with confession is repentance, Nehemiah in 1:8-9 reminds God of a promise that if the Jewish people will return to God and obey God's commandments, God will return them to their home even if they are scattered to the farthest corner of the earth.

Nehemiah Principle Three

Accountability involves asking for help and stating your needs.

The king surprises Nehemiah by responding with an unexpected question: "What is it you want?" Despite his fear, Nehemiah dares to ask the king's help. (Notice that he prays first and prefaces his request with a compliment for the king.) Then, perhaps even more surprising than the king's question is his answer to Nehemiah's request: The king says "yes." So, Nehemiah gets to go home. When you confront your fears, ask for help, and clearly state your needs, you may be surprised at the result.

When we think about it the word "need" is often used when we really mean the word "should." It is common for many to say, "I need to pray more," or "I need to make more calls to those in group." Those are not "needs;" they are "shoulds." Expressing a need is really asking for help. We all have rather large and universal needs. Years ago my wife and I asked ourselves what needs God created inside all of us. We knew that God created "male and female" in "his own image" (Gen. 1:27). Since men and women are made in God's image, we felt they must have many things in common. So believing that men and women have the same universal needs, we also felt that many of us don't always get those needs met as we grow up and that we learn to cope with that lack of fulfillment.

If you are going to be accountable, in order to do so, you should know what the big needs or desires are. As I list them, try to think about your own life. Ask yourself how well you did about getting them met in childhood and later in life. If you didn't get them met, ask yourself how you learned to cope with that.

Our universal needs are:
to be heard and understood,
affirmed, blessed, safe, touched, chosen and included.

Nehemiah Principle Four

The journey of healing is never traveled alone.
You will need the army around you.

Nehemiah asks also for some letters of reference that will give safe passage through the territories on the way to Jerusalem. With those letters in hand, he's ready to go. Nehemiah plans to travel alone almost 1,000 miles through territory occupied by many enemies of the Jews. But the king is wiser, and he keeps Nehemiah from making one of the great mistakes that many of us also make. We frequently imitate Nehemiah, who thought he could take this enormous journey alone. The king, however, sent army officers and cavalry to accompany Nehemiah (chapter 2, verse 9). Remember, you must not attempt a journey of transformation alone. Our "army" can be found in our L.I.F.E. Recovery Group. These are men or women who are willing to stand with us against the attack. I've never known anyone who has changed a negative behavior on his or her own or even with the help of only one accountability partner. You must be willing to go to any length, geographically, emotionally and logically to find your "army officers and cavalry."

Nehemiah Principle Five

Accountability assumes that the enemy wants to defeat us,
especially when we start trying to do the right thing.

In verse 10 of chapter two, it's clear that the enemies of Israel don't like any thought of rebuilding projects. There are vital analogies throughout this book, and this is an important one. So many Christians assume that when they start a healing process and seek to return to the Lord, their lives will automatically get better. We may think we'll be spared the consequences of our behavior because we've committed to change. We hope our new way of life erases the results of the old. This passage from Nehemiah reminds us that Satan hates our intention to do the right thing and to rebuild. In I Peter 5:8, Peter compares Satan to a lion roaming around and waiting to devour his prey. Nehemiah's journey home is symbolic of our journey when we want to return to our home in God. Satan doesn't want us to make that journey. He is going to attack us. Satan knows the places in our lives where we are most vulnerable. He has countless forms and tells innumerable lies.

Nehemiah Principle Six

In the face of overwhelming discouragement and damage, rebuilding may simply be a matter of just getting started.

When Nehemiah gets home to Jerusalem, the end of chapter two describes that he goes out at night to survey the damage. It must have been like looking at Ground Zero after the World Trade Center was destroyed by terrorists. What a terrible sight! The analogy here is that for many of us who seek healing, we might suddenly wake up to all the damage we've created around us. This realization can be extremely discouraging. The enormity of the rebuilding task can be daunting. We may feel paralyzed and not know how or where to start to rebuild. In AA language, Nehemiah does "the next right thing." He simply gathers everyone and non-dramatically says, "Let's start rebuilding."

(At the end of chapter two the enemies present themselves again. Nehemiah reminds everyone that God is in control and that they belong to Him. He says that the enemies have no historic claim to the people of God. In like fashion, when you're under attack, remind yourself that Satan has no claim on your life if you're a believer in Christ.)

The next section is an outline of the specific way Nehemiah starts his enormous job. Chapter three, on the surface, is a hard one with its long list of difficult names. However, the chapter is a wonderful example of organization. Nehemiah divides the work into small segments and various groups accept responsibility for each piece.

The division of labor outlined in Nehemiah Three isn't a unique principle. This age-old wisdom reminds us that if we look at the whole project of pursuing recovery, we may feel overwhelmed. But when we simply start building and focus on the immediate task at hand, we ultimately will reach our goal. The great AA phrase "one day at a time" certainly applies. Despite the damage and the discouragement, the first step of transformation is to simply get started.

Nehemiah Principle Seven

Accountability requires getting the garbage out of your life.

Hidden in the verses of chapter three are two great principles. Verse 14 reports that Malkijah repairs the Dung Gate. (That term is the NIV translation. Substitute your own word - garbage, manure, or whatever suits you). Jerusalem had many gates and each one had a function. Obviously, the Dung Gate was the gate that channeled the garbage and refuse out of the city. It was the sanitation gate, which was vital or else the city would choke on its own filth. If you've ever been in a city that was having a garbage strike, you'll understand the importance of the Dung Gate. Many health experts believe that the greatest advance of the

20th century was the widespread use of sanitation. This modern practice is responsible for ridding the world of more filth and disease than any other medical advance.

One analogy applicable here is that you might feel sometimes that your lot in life has involved dealing with dung. You get the worst assignments, the unimportant tasks, etc. An important principle from Nehemiah is that sometimes what seems like the filthy project might be the most important one.

There's another important point about the Dung Gate: What is the filth in your life? What do you need to get rid of? Think about Paraphernalia Garbage, those contributing objects or materials involved with your coping. Let's first remember that you are trying to change a particular behavior. When you think about that behavior, ask yourself if there are any objects or materials that contribute to that behavior. For example, a smoker would have a lighter or ashtrays around the house. If you drink too much, get rid of the alcohol in your house, office or even in your car. Maybe you eat too much. Are there certain foods in your house you need to get rid of? Be relentless. Maybe it's to throw away a stash of pornography, remove Internet access from your computer, cancel cable service to your home, or say goodbye to an affair partner.

All behavior has a backstory – a series of events and circumstances that led up to it. In the field of addiction we call this series of events a ritual. All behaviors start with a thought about doing the behavior. The thought is usually triggered by some event, interaction, or stimulus. Perhaps it is a stressful event at work, an argument with a spouse, or a perceived rejection of some kind. We sometimes call these thoughts preoccupations, fantasies, or obsessions if we spend hours every day just thinking about the behavior.

Don't forget that there may be emotions you need to deal with as part of the garbage of your life. This "dung" could be anger, resentments, or jealousy. It could be deep hurts from old memories. These may take longer to work on, but don't ignore the feelings you need to deal with. Pride is garbage. Pride is about pain, fear and sadness. As we already know, garbage stinks and we need to get rid of it. This is really true when it comes to thoughts that pollute our brains. There are different types of "stinking thinking." Let's list several of them for you here: delusions, rationalizations and lies. So accountability will remind us that every behavior, object, excuse or lie that is a part of the ritual must also be stopped.

Nehemiah Principle Eight

Accountability means building close to home.

Look at verses 23 and 30 of chapter three and note that these people made repairs to the parts of the walls that were across from or next to their own houses. This is an important point. So many of us get into "global thinking" when we embrace the healing journey. We want to rush out and tell the world about the new and helpful things we're learning. Before recovery, many of us distract ourselves by helping others rather than addressing our own problems. The message of Nehemiah 3 is that we need to build close to home. Before we go off in haste to evangelize the world about recovery, we should repair the damage to our own homes, to our spouses, and to our children. "First things first" is another AA slogan, and the first rebuilding must happen at home. Before we go off too hastily, we should ask ourselves what repairs need to be made to our own homes, to our spouses and to our children.

Nehemiah Principle Nine

Accountability means preparing ahead of time for the attacks to come.

Chapter four is a vital chapter. It begins with a description of how the enemies are marshaling their energies to come against the building project. Nehemiah knows that the enemy is capable and deadly and that everyone needs to be prepared. Remember that the enemy in the story is a representation of how Satan attacks. The people could easily get discouraged by the threat. Nehemiah deals with the menace by praying and by posting a guard day and night (verse 9).

The message for recovery is clear: You can't wait for the attack to come. Instead, you must *prepare for it.* Living by this principle is a great challenge. So many men fall because they tell themselves, "When I get tempted, then I'll call someone or do something." That's your pride talking. When you get tempted, a part of the temptation is that you're lonely, angry, bored, and lustful. You probably won't feel like calling anyone then. You won't want to resist the temptation or deal with it. You may be into your juvenile feelings of entitlement and convince yourself that you "deserve" to get some of your needs met in a sinful way. *If you wait until you're in trouble before asking for help, you won't ask.* Let me state this principle another way:

> ### *We must prepare in a time of <u>strength</u>*
> ### *for the times of weakness that will surely come.*

You must prepare for the attacks against your sobriety. When you are humble and convicted enough that you want to change and to be sober, put energy into fortifying your recovery plan. Consider specifically how you'll guard your heart and position others to stand with you for protection.

Reflect back on the work you did in Principle One about your rituals. Do you remember the lists you made of behaviors you'll have to stop in order to prevent yourself from getting into your rituals? Thinking through your rituals and setting boundaries is part of preparation. Again, let me be clear:

> ### *Don't wait for temptation!*
> ### *Prepare for it, because it will come.*

Do you get the point? *What?* You think being in recovery means you've had brain surgery and all cravings have been removed? Did you think that the world has been transformed and all triggers have vanished? You think you're better than others who must work at being sober? Get humble and get prepared.

Nehemiah Principle Ten

Accountability means guarding the weakest places where you're most vulnerable.

Nehemiah chapter four describes another important strategy that applies to recovery: Not only is the guard positioned day and night, but it's also placed at the weakest places. You must be sure you have warriors standing with you in your most vulnerable places.

This isn't rocket science. Know your weak places (selfishness, tiredness and boredom) ask your accountability group to remind you to "work your program." Weaknesses can be thought of in several categories, ritual weakness, emotional weakness, spiritual weakness, physical weakness, triggers and ADHD. When you know your weaknesses and rituals and how you get most sorely tempted, make sure a number of people in your group are aware of those pitfalls. Ask them to help you prepare for those times, so that you have automatic defenses in place. How can defense happen automatically? One basic example is to call someone from your L.I.F.E. Recovery Group every day. Schedule times during the day when you know you'll talk to someone. And don't depend on your willingness to make a call. Ask them to call you if they don't hear from you by a certain time.

If during your call you practice expressing your feelings and processing any pain that has come up you will quickly strengthen your relational and intimacy skills. In another example, if you travel, a good plan for preparing upfront for possible temptations is to make sure several people know your schedule and where you're going. Arrange with them to call you at various times so that you can expect to hear from someone and not get yourself into trouble. Do you see how this strategy works?

During your L.I.F.E. Recovery Group meeting, share your weakest places of vulnerability. Ask your group to help you construct a plan that's proactive in providing defenses. Remember, if a person doesn't take their weaknesses seriously these vulnerabilities will lead to great damage from the attacks of temptation. Every weakness requires a prevention plan – phone calls, meetings and establishing ongoing boundaries.

Nehemiah Principle Eleven

Accountability is always in a group, not in only one person.

You will also notice that Nehemiah uses a lot of warriors, never just one. Warriors stand together. A powerful illustration is a scene from the movie *Gladiator*. The main character, Maximus, has been made into a slave and forced to fight as a gladiator. He's in the Coliseum, where the plan of the Romans is that he and a group of other gladiators are going to be slaughtered in a re-creation of the second battle of Carthage. Maximus gathers the men around and says to them, "Whatever comes through those gates, if we stay together, we will survive." As the Roman chariots enter the arena, the gladiators stand together, lock shields, and fend off the attack. Maximus continually exhorts them, "Stay as one." Because of their connected strength, they survive against superior odds.

That movie scene is a great picture of accountability: People standing as one, together. *Whatever the world or Satan sends your way, if you stand together with others in recovery, you can survive.*

The most common mistake concerning accountability is made by well-intentioned Christians who think that they can have an accountability "partner." This plan is foolishness. Haven't you lied skillfully enough to defeat one partner, or even two? After all, we addicts are usually great liars. We know how to get by without revealing the truth, especially if we only have to convince one person. You need a group who really know you and who won't be fooled when you're having times of weakness.

There is strength in fellowship. Loneliness is one of the reasons you acted out in the first place. *Fellowship is the answer.* Make no mistake, though, about the meaning of "fellowship." I'm defining fellowship as those who really know you. It isn't your average Bible study group or church-based class. Those in your group must <u>really</u> know everything about you – all your secret sins, your wounds, your temptations, your feelings. It's also important for them to be encouragers, and not disciplinarians. All of us respond much better to positive reinforcement.

One of my principles is that:

Fellowship equals freedom from lust.

You must identify at least four or five others who are willing to stand with you. These people should know all your acting out behaviors, all your rituals, all of the ways you've fantasized, and all of your emotional history. Checking in with them won't take long because they know you so well already. They'll quickly be able to give you feedback about what you should do to protect yourself in the days to come. These safe people will stand with you in the gap against all attacks.

Nehemiah Principle Twelve

Our motivation for transformation should be selfless.

There is a great battle cry in the fourteenth verse of chapter four. Nehemiah says, *"Don't be afraid of them [the attackers]. Remember the Lord, who is great and awesome, and fight for your brothers, your sons and your daughters, your wives and your homes."* (NIV). The great reminder here, again, is that the battle belongs to the Lord. But there's much more in this exhortation: The battle is also to be fought for others.

After the great catastrophe of September 11, 2001, we were all inspired by the example of the firefighters and police officers who sacrificed their lives in attempts to save others. That is what heroes do. That is what warriors do. You should be no different. Your motivation should be to prevent injuring anybody else around you. It should be to never again see the look of pain on the face of someone close to you, like your wife. It should be to keep your home safe for your children and others. And it should be to provide leadership and an example for your brothers who also seek to be transformed.

If your motivation is to avoid all personal consequences and if your recovery is fear based you'll probably fail. Fear only lasts so long. When it subsides, you'll be tempted to act out again. Motivation that's proactive and includes eventually helping others is usually much more successful. After you're stable in your recovery, focus your energy outward. Get out of your selfishness. Be willing to lead a life of sacrifice.

I've had the opportunity to speak to several military groups. When we think about battles and fighting wars, what do we honor in soldiers? It's that they are willing to die for their country. This willingness to sacrifice, even to the point of death, is part of what it means to be transformed. Would you be willing to die for someone beyond yourself? What about your children? Your wife? Your sisters and brothers? When you can answer "yes" to those questions, you'll be successful in your journey of transformation.

Nehemiah Principle Thirteen

Accountability means building as well as defending

Here is one last point from chapter four. Notice in verses 16 and 17 that half of the men built and half stood guard with their spears, bows, and shields. Even the men who carried material carried the supplies in one hand and a sword in the other. The picture is that there was a balance between building and defending a balance in equal measure. Those who only have a defensive strategy in place get really tired of always being on guard. It takes a lot of energy to defend all the time. Defending is only negative. It's about the things you don't do.

The challenge of this picture in Nehemiah chapter four is that we must be *building* something, not just defending. AA says; if you're going to stop something start something. We're all built to be creative and productive. We long to build. God put creative energy into our brains so that we will "be fruitful and increase in number," Gen. 1:28. Use the energy and effort that you put into acting out and put it into building and envision what you are going to build.

The real journey of transformation is about going forward in positive directions. Our healing must be proactive. It's not enough to be removing the rubble from your life, or even to be guarding against slips and relapse. Genuine and lasting transformation requires building an entire way of living life that goes far beyond your acting out behavior.

Nehemiah Principle Fourteen

Accountability means putting positive things into your life.

The program of recovery can't be about deprivation, or it will fail. Many falter in their recovery because all of their program activity is negative. Remember that you're probably an abandonment victim. A voice inside you screams for love, attention, and activity. If all you do is continue to deny these basic needs, that same voice will continue to scream – and will probably get louder. You'll remain vulnerable to the false substitutes you've historically used to meet your legitimate needs and medicate your feelings.

Positive actions are discussed in Principle Seven where we talk about asking the Lord to give you a vision. Remember some of those practical, positive steps. Examples include:

- Eating better
- Getting more rest
- Getting a medical check-up
- Exercising
- Inviting a friend for coffee
- Making a date with your spouse
- Making an appointment with a therapist or counselor
- Going to a workshop
- Getting into a Bible study
- Buying yourself some music that inspires you
- Doing anything just for fun

This isn't a complete list, but it provides some sample ideas. You'll notice that most of these items concern self-care, which is something most addicts have difficulty doing. Many of us got the false message that taking care of ourselves is "selfish." The reality is that historically you *have been* selfish, but not in this sense. You've been selfishly providing yourself with false substitutes for comfort, excitement, fun and pleasure. Part of building a healthy life is to find positive ways of meeting your needs.

Every project begins with an idea, and every idea leads to a picture of what will be built. Every artist, every builder, and every writer has always begun with the picture of the finished project in their mind. When you finish this principle I want you to have a beginning vision of what you are going to build. Here are some areas where you might consider building, physical, character, spiritual and relational. In the L.I.F.E. Recovery Group Meeting Guidelines we suggest that participants share with the group the positive steps they have been taken that week. This practice is a great encouragement and gives an opportunity for accountability during check-in.as well.

Nehemiah Principle Fifteen

Accountability is an on-going, lifelong process, but God provides sustaining energy.

Our original adrenaline that gave us so much energy for the start of the project eventually wears off. Now we come to the mundane tasks and the work can be expensive. This is when our heart and motivations are tested. Chapter five of Nehemiah reports that the work gets tiring and expensive. The strength of the workers gives out. The rebuilding costs mount, and some begin extracting taxes and expenses. However, instead of simply helping the cause, these workers are making a profit. Some of the people even go so far as to sell their own children into slavery, which was a custom of the time.

In my own first year of recovery, I went to therapy and support groups all the time. I was scared enough to go to something recovery oriented almost every day. The effort was expensive and it was tiring. I remember thinking during that time, "When does this end? When do I get to stop being an addict?" Pat Carnes discovered in some of his early research that the period between the sixth and the twelfth months of healing is the most dangerous time for relapse. I think the main reason is because early recovery is so exhausting. Another reason is because we're still facing the consequences of our addiction during the first year, and life hasn't necessarily become much better. During this time, we might be tempted to go back into slavery, back to our behaviors just to cope with our exhaustion. The vicious cycle begins again.

It's important you accept that doing the work of healing will be expensive and exhausting. Rebuilding is difficult, but God is sufficient. Don't sell yourself back into slavery.

Read chapter 5 verse 13. Nehemiah reports, *"I also shook out the folds of my robe and said, 'In this way may God shake out of His house and possessions every man who does not keep this promise. So may such a man be shaken out and emptied!' At this the whole assembly said, 'Amen,' and praised the LORD. And the people did as they had promised."*

As someone in the process of transformation, keep your promises!

This principle from Nehemiah is a reminder that when you think you can't go on - or you think you've finished your recovery work or that you're healed – realize you're not. Keep reaching out for help and support. Look further to a successful recovery model, the practices found in the LRM (L.I.F.E. Recovery Model http://www.freedomeveryday.org/lrm/index.php) to help you re-evaluate your recovery plan or take begin giving back, sharing your story and serving those still caught in the trap of addiction.

On the day I am writing this I had breakfast with a longtime friend of mine who has been sober now for 20 years. He told me about a new meeting that he had just started and that he was going back to all the basics of doing all the work all over again. This is a healthy way of life, and he doesn't plan to change a thing. I know that maintaining fellowship and accountability are crucial to my own journey. Be sure to watch against falling into the dangerous trap of thinking you've "made it," are "healed," or can now "let down your guard." When it comes to change and healing, do whatever it takes, however much it costs, and God will find a way. The biblical wisdom portrayed here is that when a person isn't greedy or selfish, God does provide, a theme reiterated in many other parts of the Bible.

Nehemiah Principle Sixteen

When tempted, remain committed to transformation without wavering.

In Nehemiah chapter six, the wall is nearing completion. The enemies are frustrated with the results of their frontal assaults, so they come up with three different schemes to defeat the rebuilding project. True to the "cunning" nature of addiction (and Satan), these attacks are much more subtle.

First, the enemies invite Nehemiah to a meeting outside of the city to talk about their differences. But instead of this reasonable-sounding plan, they actually are plotting to kill. This scheme is the plot of 'distraction." The enemies are being polite and civil, and it might seem rational to have a meeting. It's tempting to ignore the potential consequences of getting involved with the enemy, especially if you believe you have a "good" reason. Rest assured that the enemies of transformation have a hidden (and evil) agenda. Understand that Satan will come after you with very subtle, civil, and rational sounding distractions. It may simply be something like, "You've been working so hard, why not take a break? Have a little fun." Or perhaps Satan deceives you through your own self-talk: "I'm tired. Why do I have to spend so much energy working my program? I have such restrictive boundaries maybe I can relax them a little." You may be tempted to stop thinking of yourself as an "addict" and decide you've gotten beyond your earlier temptations. Maybe it's okay to (------ *fill in the blank*) without accountability if you're only going to (------ *fill in the blank*). Or surely by now you can handle (------ *fill in the blank*) after all, you have a legitimate reason to (------ *fill in the blank*). Do you see how easy it can be to justify behavior?

I remember when I came out of treatment and my brother knew I had changed, he said to me, "Mark, when can we be a normal family again?" The answer to that is, "Hopefully, never." In other words, "I'm not coming down from the wall."

Temptation comes in many disguises and many voices, including your own. Remember, you're dealing with spiritual warfare. Hear the battle cry of Nehemiah: "I am carrying on a great project and cannot come down." It's not a complicated decision he ponders over. Your work is important. Don't let the enemy distract you. Nehemiah is a man of persistence, fortitude and simplicity. Take his example to heart. Don't lose sight of the great work you're doing, and never waiver from your commitment to transformation.

Nehemiah Principle Seventeen

Transformation targets you for rumors and personal attacks.

The enemies step up the attack as chapter six unfolds. In the second scheme, they circulate a rumor that Nehemiah is trying to usurp the power of the king. The enemies are basically accusing him of grandiosity. They claim Nehemiah is trying to be too powerful and is too full of himself. They suggest he come to the meeting (outside the city, remember) and discuss his intentions.

Be aware that your journey of transformation will target you for rumors. Some of the attacking voices will come from the religious folk. People may accuse you of trying to be something that you're not, or condemn you for being "selfish" in making healthy choices. They may question your participation in a support group program. Other attacking voices will be secular ones. They'll taunt you for being "self-righteous" about your morals. Don't be surprised if you're accused of being "judgmental" for maintaining standards for healthy intimacy. People from both religious and secular communities will wonder about your recovery program in general and believe you're trying to escape responsibility by hiding behind an "addiction."

In an article in *Playboy* magazine, I was accused (along with others) of inventing the concept of sexual addiction so that "professionals" could make money treating it. The assumption was that sexual addiction doesn't exist. In another instance a former colleague of mine who was jealous of my success accused me of having an affair with another colleague. All of it was not true but for some who heard it, like those at a large national ministry, the damage is still something I'm trying to overcome. You don't know how many times the words of Nehemiah come to me: *"You are just making it up out of your head."* These rumors and attacks can get really tiring and sometimes frightening. You will often be misunderstood about your feelings and motivations as you seek to be transformed into a closer image of Christ.

These false accusations against Nehemiah are the same kind of rumors that Jewish leaders circulated about Jesus. They said He was trying to be King. They dragged Him in front of Pilate and accused Him of being a radical and a revolutionary. Pilate knew these charges were crazy and thought he could resolve the problem when he stood Jesus next to Barabbas and asked the people their choice of whom he should release. Barabbas was a known revolutionary, and Pilate must have thought this solution was a way to *"wash his hands"* of the matter and get the people to do his work for him. Of course, Pilate's plan backfired to Jesus' ultimate glory and our eternal salvation.

The point is that you'll deal with misunderstanding and perhaps false rumors. It's easy to get distracted by trying to explain yourself. I, at least, tend to get defensive, which only robs me of energy I need to focus on my work of transformation. Nehemiah provides a better example of how to deal with this kind of attack. He says to his accusers, *"Nothing like what you're saying is happening; you are just making it up out of your head"* (verse 8). Nehemiah responds simply and directly, and then he quickly gets back to work.

He is, though, in touch with his emotions regarding this attack. He recognizes the enemies are trying to frighten him and the others. The attackers hope, *"Their hands will get too weak for the work, and it will not be completed"* (verse 9). Nehemiah prays that God will "strengthen my hands" as he leads the people. At times you'll need to pray for strength and ask supportive friends to encourage you in the ongoing work.

You do not have to be fully understood to pursue your "great work" of transformation. You may be falsely accused of pride, arrogance, ambition, or selfishness. You may be stung by rumors. You'll certainly feel distracted and discouraged. You'll fear your hands are too weak for their work. Consider Nehemiah's response and renew your courage and commitment.

Nehemiah Principle Eighteen

Transformation results in a willingness to sacrifice even your own life.

The truth of the situation is that the work is very dangerous. There is one final plot. An invalid by the name of Shemaiah invites Nehemiah to come with him to the temple where they will be safe. The work is dangerous he says, and if Nehemiah is going to continue his good effort of rebuilding the wall, he must stay safe. Nehemiah's response is powerful: "Should a man like me run away or try to save his own life?"

As you seek to build and lead a transformed life, at times you'll be tempted to retreat to safety. Others may even encourage you to take the easy path of self-protection. For example, when you're being successful in living a pure life and are finding opportunities to share the message about God's transforming power, you may be tempted (or advised) not to share your story because it might harm your reputation. I had many people try to convince me to stop traveling after the terrorist attack on September 11, 2002. In a variety of ways you may be pressured to stop your important work.

Nehemiah, though, wisely discerned that Shemaiah was no true friend out to protect his best interest. He knew that Shemaiah actually was in on a plot to kill him inside the supposed safety of the temple itself. My guess is that Nehemiah's response would have been the same even if he wasn't aware of Shemaiah's true intentions. Nehemiah would have refused to retreat from his mission.

For those of us who seek to change and heal, often the work will seem very dangerous too. It will feel at times that we must take a certain amount of risk to do the new behaviors we have been told will heal us. For one thing, when we learn how to start telling the truth to others, we will confront the anxiety that gets us to think "if they really knew me, they would hate me or leave me." Maybe for you it will mean having the courage to go to L.I.F.E. Recovery Group or confessing your sins to spiritual authority. I have often been amazed at how courageous those in recovery have been who resign and find another job, perhaps for less money, because it provides them with more time at home and more safety.

Our response must be the same. In Ephesians 5:1-2, Paul says we should be "imitators" of God and be willing, like Christ, to give ourselves up as a "fragrant offering and sacrifice to God." Sacrifice can mean taking risks to do the right thing, even if it makes us feel afraid. Obviously, we won't be perfect at courageously continuing in our work, no matter the risk. Only Jesus was perfectly self-sacrificing. But we can draw strength from His example, face our fears, and ignore the voices that suggest we abandon our work.

Accountability will mean our accountability partners will often need to remind us that the enemy sends false messages and plots and schemes to get us away from the work. Accountability reminds you to stay on the wall! There is a constant theme in both Nehemiah 5 and 6. Nehemiah is willing to do whatever it takes as long as it takes. Undoubtedly he is tired and frightened, but at every temptation, every problem that arises, and every distraction to stay focused on the task, he stays on the wall.

Although the wall is finished, the work inside the city is just beginning. Recovery is building healthy boundaries so that the enemy will have a much harder time attacking us. These Principles establish those boundaries. Those boundaries are the beginning. Now you face the lifelong interior work you must do. That will affect your family and all your relationships. You will rebuild your house, and your legacy will be great.

Tying It All Together

I have gone to such length to teach these 18 principles from Nehemiah because I believe they provide a wonderful example of the total process of living in freedom everyday. This story of humility, courage, action, focus, and dependence on God illustrates the Seven Principles outlined in this L.I.F.E. Recovery Guide. Rebuilding the wall is a picture of transforming your life. This process involves surrender on a daily basis. Regardless of the challenges, whether from within your own heart or from external sources, being transformed means surrendering your life, your will, and the outcomes to God.

Taking life one day at a time and maintaining accountability will be the core of your program for the rest of your life. This reality isn't just because you're an addict. It's because you are someone who seeks to follow Christ.

Time is God's

Before we finish with Nehemiah, notice a statement at the end of chapter six. How long do you think the building project takes? A dozen years? Maybe only eight to ten years? Surely such a huge project takes three or four years, at least, right?

Wrong. Verse 15 reports, "So the wall was completed on the 25th of Elul, in 52 days. When all our enemies heard about this, all the surrounding nations were afraid and lost their self-confidence, because they realized that this work had been done with the help of our God." Did you catch that? *The wall was finished in only 52 days*!

In one sense, the process of transformation is a lifelong endeavor. We're never "finished" with the journey of becoming transformed into a sacrificial life in Christ. We continually must be about the task of rebuilding the walls – of our hearts, our lives, our families, and our relationship with Christ.

But in another sense, the intensity of the work will not last as long as you may fear. It won't always be as hard as it is in the beginning. The struggle to maintain sobriety will ease. Integrity will take the place of dishonesty. The pain of the past will recede. Relationships will be restored. Wounds will heal. Fellowship and community will replace loneliness. You'll discover you've even been surprised by joy – that your spirit knows a peace that passes understanding.

Another great slogan from Alcoholics Anonymous is found in the "Promises of Recovery." After listing a variety of positives, the recovering person will experience, the "*Big Book*," which gives a timeframe for when these promises will be fulfilled: "before you're half way through" of the first intense part of your journey, perhaps after only 52 days.

During those times when you're tired and lonely and frightened, remember Nehemiah's story and be encouraged by his example. You, too, are doing a great work as you build a life of purity, and good things may start coming to you in a shorter time than you might imagine.

Time belongs to God, and He will guide your journey from beginning to end.

RESOURCES

No Stones: Women Redeemed from Sexual Addiction, (2nd edition), Marnie C. Ferree, Downers Grove, IL: InterVarsity Press, 2010.

Healing the Wounds of Sexual Addiction, Mark Laaser, Grand Rapids, MI: Zondervan, 2004. ISBN 0-310-25657-7.

Pornography Trap, Ralph Earle & Mark Laaser, Kansas City: Beacon Hill Press, 2002. ISBN 0-8341-1938-2.

A number of other good resources are available to aid Christians in their journey of transformation. Through both printed material and the World Wide Web, those who seek to live in freedom everyday can find information and inspiration.

Because it's impossible to maintain an up-to-date list of resources in this printed *L.I.F.E. Guide*, visit these websites for current suggestions of where to turn for help in the areas of addiction, co-addiction, trauma, and recovery:

www.freedomeveryday.org

www.bethesdaworkshops.org

www.faithfulandtrueministries.com

(Printed copies of resource lists are also available through Bethesda Workshops for those who don't have Internet access.)

ABOUT THE AUTHOR

Marnie C. Ferree, M.A., is a licensed marriage and family therapist in Nashville, Tennessee, where she directs Bethesda Workshops, a clinical intensive treatment program (a 501(c)(3) non-profit organization) for sex addicts, their spouses, and sexually addicted couples. The workshop program for female sex addicts, established in 1997, was the first of its kind in the country and today draws participants from across the U. S. and Canada.

Marnie is frequent lecturer at professional and recovery conferences, churches, and schools. She also consults with individuals and churches, especially when a church leader is involved in sexual sin. Marnie is a member of the American Association of Christian Counselors, the Society for the Advancement of Sexual Health (SASH), and a clinical fellow in the American Association of Marriage and Family Therapists. She is also a Certified Sex Addiction Therapist (CSAT) through the International Institute for Trauma and Addiction Professionals (IITAP), which is the premier certifying body in the field.

Marnie has published dozens of articles in a variety of professional journals, magazines and newspapers. Marnie's book, *No Stones: Women Redeemed from Sexual Addiction* , about women's recovery from sexual abuse and addiction, was published in a second edition by InterVarsity Press in 2010. She is also the editor and a contributing writer for *Making Advances - A Comprehensive Guide for Treating Female Sex and Love Addicts*, which is a clinical textbook for professionals.

To Order *No Stones*:

Call toll-free **866-464-4325**

Or order on-line at **www.BethesdaWorkshops.org**

To Contact Marnie:

Call 615-467-5610

Or send email to mferree@bethesdaworkshops.org

BETHESDA WORKSHOPS

- a place for healing from sexual addiction-

Mission and Vision

Bethesda Workshops encourages sexual wholeness by ministering to those damaged by sexual abuse, sin, and addiction. We provide a place of healing where people can begin a process of restoration with God, with themselves, with others, and within their marriages. We use the best clinical strategies, coupled with Christian principles, to achieve spiritual, emotional, behavioral, and relational healing.

Services

Intensive workshops are offered for sexual addiction recovery. Most workshops are 4 days and are held Wednesday through Saturday. Clinical intensives include:

Healing for Men	- for male sexual addicts
Healing for Women	- for female sexual addicts
Healing for Partners	- for spouses and partners of addicts
Healing for Couples	- for addict/coaddict couples

Contact Information

Bethesda Workshops
3710 Franklin Rd.
Nashville, TN 37204
615-467-5610

www.bethesdaworkshops.org

Toll-free 866-464-HEAL

L.I.F.E. RECOVERY INTERNATIONAL
- Living In Freedom Everyday -

Mission

The mission of L.I.F.E. Recovery International is to encourage, empower and equip God's people to live everyday in sexual integrity. L.I.F.E. Recovery works with church leadership to offer hurting people within local congregations a safe place to confront sexual addiction and brokenness and to walk in Christ's unconditional love.

Services

L.I.F.E. Recovery offers Christ-centered and relationally oriented support groups that incorporate spiritual discipline, small group accountability, and ongoing prayer and support for those struggling with sexual brokenness. L.I.F.E. also provides recovery materials and training for support group leaders.

Ministry Leaders

Johna Hale, M.A. and Bob Hale

Contact Information

L.I.F.E. Recovery International
P.O. Box 952317
Lake Mary, FL 32795

www.freedomeveryday.org

Toll-free 866-408-LIFE

Made in the USA
Las Vegas, NV
23 June 2021